The ULTIMATE Vegetarian COLLECTION

It's All Good!
International Recipes

Autumn House® Publishing
www.autumnhousepublishing.com
A Division of **REVIEW AND HERALD® PUBLISHING**
Since 1861

Published by Autumn House® Publishing, a division of Review and Herald® Publishing,
Hagerstown, MD 21741-1119

This book was
Edited by Shirley Mulkern
Copyedited by James Cavil
Designed by Ron J. Pride
Layout support by Tina Ivany, Heather Rogers, and Patricia Wegh
Typeset: Rockwell 10/13; Univers 57 Condensed 10/11

Photography:
Joel D. Springer
David R. Smith
IClub
PhotoDisc
© 2008 Jupiterimages Corporation, pps. 11, 33, 42, 49, 69, 73, 88
© iStockphoto.com/Kelly Cline, p. 4/Ivan Mateev, p. 123, 132

Contributors:
Juanita Alexander
Ruth Davis
Barbara Frazier
Johnetta Frazier
Christina Fleming-Gabriel
Donna Green Goodman
Pat Humphrey
Jocelyn M. Peterson
Donna A. Smith
Erma Williams
Pamela Avonne Williams

Special thanks to Jason McCracken

Library of Congress Cataloging-in-Publication Data

It's all good : international recipes.
          p. cm.—(Ultimate vegetarian collection)
1. Vegetarian cookery. 2. Cookery, International. I. Autumn House Publishing.
     TX837.I74 2008
     641.5'636--dc22
                              2008005140

ISBN 978-0-8127-0483-9

To order **It's All Good!**, call **1-800-765-6955**.

Visit us at **www.AutumnHousePublishing.com** for information on other Autumn House® products.

Contents

Introduction

Today, everywhere you turn, somebody's talking about health. The messages come through loud and clear: Lower your fat and salt intake, watch your cholesterol, eat more fiber, get plenty of exercise—and the list goes on. Maybe you're thinking, *In theory, it all sounds good, but putting these things into practice—well, that's another story.* Many people think that in order to eat healthfully, you have to always shop at health food stores and spend a lot of time preparing fancy dishes. But that's not necessarily so. The good news is you can find natural, healthful foods right in your neighborhood grocery store. And preparing them is both easy and fun.

For over 50 years, *Message* magazine has featured "Food for Health," a section devoted to health-conscious vegetarian recipes. Why? Because we think eating healthfully is just as important as your spiritual health. Science has confirmed that a plant-based diet can help to prevent and heal many chronic illnesses. The diet that God originally designed for us to eat could be the key in helping you to feel better. So start today by including more grains, fruits, and vegetables in your diet (and lots of soy). Eat a raw salad every day. Season with garlic, onions, and fresh herbs like parsley, sage, rosemary, thyme, basil, cilantro, oregano, and dill. Then get ready to feel really great!

If you're like most of us, you don't have a lot of time to spend in the kitchen. And even if you did, you'd probably rather spend your time doing other things. So preparing nutritious meals in a hurry can be a challenge. These recipes are designed to help you meet that challenge quickly and healthfully.

Some recipes will allow you the flexibility of preparing and freezing meals for use at a later date. They also make excellent leftovers. Many of these dishes use a minimal number of ingredients to save time, but are maximum in flavor.

We hope you enjoy the recipes and your free time away from the kitchen!

–The Editors, *Message* Magazine

Special Ingredients

Most of the ingredients listed in these recipes are available at your neighborhood supermarket. However, a few special items may need to be purchased at a health food store. Here's a list of some of the more unfamiliar ingredients and where to buy them.

Commercial Vegetarian Products

These products are sold in Super Wal-Marts, Adventist Book Centers, and many grocery stores:

- Loma Linda Foods, canned or frozen
- Morningstar Farms, frozen
- Worthington Foods, canned or frozen
- Yves Foods, produce section

Dry Ingredients

- G. Washington's Seasoning and Broth (Rich Brown and Golden)

Health Foods

These products can be purchased at health food stores or Asian/Mexican specialty stores.

- Bakon Seasoning (smoke flavor)
- Bragg Liquid Aminos (soy sauce substitute)
- Fakin' Bacon
- McKay's Beef Style Broth and Seasoning (Abbreviated: "McKay's Beef Style Seasoning")
- McKay's Chicken Style Broth and Seasoning (Abbreviated: "McKay's Chicken Style Seasoning")
- Nayonnaise
- Soya Kaas cheddar style cheese
- Spike Seasoning
- Vege-Sal
- Vegeit

Cooking Measurement Equivalents

1 tablespoon (tbsp) = 3 teaspoons (tsp)
$\frac{1}{16}$ cup = 1 tablespoon
$\frac{1}{4}$ cup = 2 tablespoons
$\frac{1}{6}$ cup = 2 tablespoons + 2 teaspoons
$\frac{1}{4}$ cup = 4 tablespoons
$\frac{1}{3}$ cup = 5 tablespoons + 1 teaspoon
$\frac{3}{8}$ cup = 6 tablespoons
$\frac{1}{2}$ cup = 8 tablespoons
$\frac{2}{3}$ cup = 10 tablespoons + 2 teaspoons
$\frac{3}{4}$ cup = 12 tablespoons

1 cup = 48 teaspoons
1 cup = 16 tablespoons
8 fluid ounces (fl oz) = 1 cup
1 pint (pt) = 2 cups
1 quart (qt) = 2 pints
4 cups = 1 quart
1 gallon (gal) = 4 quarts
16 ounces (oz) = 1 pound (lb)
1 milliliter (ml) = 1 cubic centimeter (cc)
1 inch (in) = 2.54 centimeters (cm)

Source: United States Department of Agriculture (USDA).

U.S.–Metric Cooking Conversions

U.S. to Metric

Capacity
$\frac{1}{5}$ teaspoon = 1 milliliter
1 teaspoon = 5 ml
1 tablespoon = 15 ml
1 fluid oz = 30 ml
$\frac{1}{5}$ cup = 47 ml
1 cup = 237 ml
2 cups (1 pint) = 473 ml
4 cups (1 quart) = .95 liter
4 quarts (1 gal.) = 3.8 liters

Weight
1 oz = 28 grams
1 pound = 454 grams

Metric to U.S.

Capacity
1 milliliter = $\frac{1}{5}$ teaspoon
5 ml = 1 teaspoon
15 ml = 1 tablespoon
100 ml = 3.4 fluid oz
240 ml = 1 cup
1 liter = 34 fluid oz
= 4.2 cups
= 2.1 pints
= 1.06 quarts
= 0.26 gallon

Weight
1 gram = .035 ounce
100 grams = 3.5 ounces
500 grams = 1.10 pounds
1 kilogram = 2.205 pounds
= 35 ounces

Breakfast

Breakfast is the most important meal of the day. Try scrambled tofu, pecan patties, tofu fried rice, or sautéed burger potatoes for breakfast. These dishes will give you the energy you need to begin your day. Research shows that students who eat a wholesome breakfast perform better in their studies than those who have little or no breakfast. Improve your breakfast habits and experience a significant difference.

Fresh Fruit Compote
• RUTH DAVIS

    1 cup fresh strawberries
    1 cup fresh pineapple chunks
    1 cup honeydew melon cubes
    2 peeled, sliced bananas
    1 cup fresh orange juice

Wash and dice strawberries, pineapple, and honeydew melon. Peel bananas and slice. Mix ingredients in a bowl and add the freshly squeezed orange juice.
Makes 4 servings. 153 calories, 0.62 g fat, 6.2 mg sodium.

Honey Prune Compote
• DONNA A. SMITH

    1 12-ounce package pitted prunes (2 cups)
    ½ cup canned sliced peaches (juice pack)
    ½ cup orange juice
    ¼ cup water
    2 tablespoons honey
    1 cinnamon stick
    1 medium orange, peeled and cut into sections

In a medium size saucepan bring prunes, peaches, orange juice, and water to a boil. Pour into medium size bowl. Stir in honey and cinnamon stick. Add orange sections and stir gently. Cool and discard cinnamon stick. Refrigerate before serving.
Makes 6 servings. 198 calories, 0 g fat, 5 mg sodium.

Almond French-Style Toast
• JOCELYN M. PETERSON

    1 cup water
    ½ cup blanched almonds
    2 dates
    2 tablespoons whole wheat flour
    1 teaspoon McKay's Chicken Style Seasoning (optional)
    8 slices dry whole wheat bread

Place all ingredients except bread in blender; whiz until smooth. Dip whole wheat bread slices into mixture. Place on lightly oiled cookie sheet and bake at 350° F for 10 minutes; then broil on both sides to a golden brown. (Or brown delicately on both sides in lightly oiled skillet over low heat.) Serve with a simple topping such as applesauce or apricot puree.
Makes 8 servings. 250 calories, 8 g fat, 180 mg sodium.

Serve a Sunday brunch buffet-style, featuring entertainment by local gospel artists. Fellowship with believers is the key ingredient. Host your own "gospel brunch"—potluck style—season and try these delightful recipes.

Fruit French Toast
• RUTH DAVIS

- 1 banana, peeled
- ½ cup fresh or frozen strawberries
- ⅓ cup apple juice
- 4 slices whole wheat bread

Blend the banana, strawberries, and apple juice together. Dip the bread in the fruit mixture. Cook on both sides on lightly oiled or nonstick griddle until lightly brown.

Makes 4 servings. 102.5 calories, 1.45 g fat, 181 mg sodium.

MENU SUGGESTION: **Serve with vegetarian breakfast links.**

Honeyed Grapefruit
• JOHNETTA FRAZIER

- 3 grapefruit
- ¼ cup honey

Cut grapefruit in half and remove seeds and core. Drizzle honey on top of each half. Garnish center of fruit with a strawberry, grape, or cherry.

Makes 6 servings. 88 calories, 0 g fat, 0 mg sodium.

Power Oats
• BARBARA FRAZIER

- 2 cups quick oats
- 8 tablespoons reduced fat peanut butter
- 1⅓ cups raisins
- 1 teaspoon vanilla

Prepare oats using package directions, but omit salt. Cook to desired consistency and stir in peanut butter, raisins, and vanilla until well mixed. Serve immediately.

Makes 6 servings. 174 calories, 8.9 g fat, 6.6 g protein, 159 mg sodium.

Oatmeal Banana Raisin Delight
• RUTH DAVIS

- 1 cup rolled oats
- 2 cups water
- 1 cup soy milk
- 2 bananas, sliced
- ½ cup raisins

Place rolled oats and water in a microwavable bowl. Microwave on high for 4 minutes and 10 seconds (or cook in a pot on stove until thickened). Add soy milk, sliced bananas, and raisins. Serve in individual bowls.

Makes 4 servings. 41.8 calories, 0.46 g fat, 33.2 mg sodium.

Simply Granola
• JOCELYN M. PETERSON

- 4 cups rolled oats
- 1 cup oat bran
- 1 cup wheat germ
- ½ cup sliced almonds or walnuts
- ¼ cup olive oil
- 1 teaspoon vanilla (or desired flavoring)
- 1 cup water
- ¾ cup honey

Combine the rolled oats, oat bran, wheat germ, and sliced almonds in a bowl. Mix the olive oil, vanilla, water, and honey in a separate container. Stir the liquid ingredients into the bowl with the dry ingredients; mix thoroughly. Spread evenly on a cookie sheet and bake in a preheated oven at 300° F for about 45 minutes, stirring every 10 minutes until baked.

Makes 12 servings. 250 calories, 5 g fat, 50 mg sodium.

Homemade Granola
• DONNA GREEN GOODMAN

    6 cups rolled oats
    4 cups quick oats
    1 cup whole wheat pastry flour
  ½ cup coconut
  ½ cup chopped nuts
  ½ cup water
  ½ cup canola oil
  ½ cup honey
    1 tablespoon alcohol-free vanilla flavoring
    1 tablespoon alcohol-free almond flavoring
 1½ teaspoons salt
      Dried fruit (optional)

Mix oats, flour, coconut, and chopped nuts thoroughly. Blend water, oil, honey, vanilla flavoring, almond flavoring, and salt in separate bowl. Add blended ingredients to mix and work with fingers until mixture is moistened and evenly mixed. Spread on large cookie sheet(s). Bake at 350° F for 1½ hours. Stir occasionally and bake until uniformly golden. Cool thoroughly. Store in airtight containers.
Makes 15 servings. 312 calories, 15 g fat, 219 mg sodium.

Apple Crunch Granola
• PAMELA AND ERMA WILLIAMS

  ½ cup chopped dried apples
  ½ cup raisins
    1 cup apple juice
    4 cups uncooked rolled oats
  ½ cup shredded coconut, unsweetened
  ⅓ cup sesame seeds
  ⅓ cup sunflower seeds
  ½ cup soy nuts
  ¼ cup soy milk powder
  ¼ cup wheat germ
  ½ cup oat bran
    1 teaspoon cinnamon
  ½ cup chopped pecans

Preheat oven to 250° F. Soak the raisins and apples for an hour or two. Combine dry ingredients in a bowl. Pour juice from the soaked raisins and apples over the oat mixture and stir to moisten the grains. Spread mixture on two cookie sheets sprayed with nonstick baking spray or lined with parchment paper. Bake for 1 hour, stirring every 10 minutes. Add the soaked raisins and apples, turn off the heat, and leave the mixture in the oven for another 15 minutes. (It should be very dry.)
Makes 14 servings. 215 calories, 12 g fat.

Breakfast Porridge (Africa)
• PAMELA WILLIAMS

    1 cup white cornmeal
    2 cups water
  ⅛ teaspoon salt
  ½ cup rice milk
  ⅓ cup water
    2 tablespoon honey
    1 teaspoon vanilla
      Nutmeg to taste
      Cinnamon to taste
      Unsweetened coconut, shredded

Mix cornmeal with just enough water to make thick paste. Bring the remaining water to a boil. Add cornmeal paste. Cook for 7 to 10 minutes. Mix the rice milk with ⅓ cup water. Add porridge, honey, vanilla, nutmeg, and cinnamon. Pour into bowl and garnish with coconut.
Makes 4 servings. 113 calories, 1 g fat, 222 mg sodium.

Breakfast Crisps

• PAMELA AND ERMA WILLIAMS

> 1 cup fine cornmeal
> ½ cup cake flour
> ½ cup coconut, shredded
> 1 teaspoon salt
> 1 tablespoon brown sugar
> 1½ tablespoons oil
> 1½ tablespoons butter
> ⅓ cup whole wheat flour, sifted
> ½ cup water

Mix ingredients and add ½ cup water. Spray cookie sheet with Pam. Pat out mixture on cookie sheet with back of spoon until about ¼-inch thick. Cut into 2-inch squares. Bake at 350° F for 25 minutes or until lightly brown.
Makes 6 servings. 182 calories, 10 g fat.

Tasty Tidbit:

Gourmet Toast

Apple: Arrange sliced apple on each piece of cinnamon toast. Drizzle with honey and broil until honey bubbles.

Bananas: Arrange sliced banana on each piece of nut bread or toast. Drizzle with honey and broil until honey bubbles.

Pecan/Walnut: Toast bread on one side. Spread untoasted side with a thin layer of butter and honey. Top with crushed pecans or walnuts and broil until brown.

• PAMELA AND ERMA WILLIAMS

Pineapple Breakfast Cookies

• RUTH DAVIS

> ½ cup vegetable oil (olive)
> ¼ cup honey
> 1 teaspoon vanilla
> ½ teaspoon salt
> ¾ cup raisins
> 1 cup pineapple, canned and drained
> 1 cup quick oats
> 1 cup whole wheat flour

Mix oil, honey, vanilla, salt, raisins, and pineapple. Add oats and flour and mix with fork. Place on oiled cookie sheet with a spoon. Bake at 350° F for 25-30 minutes.
Makes 30 servings. 80 calories, 0.63 g fat, 44 mg sodium.

Pecan Pancakes

• RUTH DAVIS

> 2 cups whole wheat flour
> 2 tablespoons egg substitute
> 2 teaspoon low-sodium baking powder
> ½ teaspoon baking soda
> ½ cup pecans, chopped
> ¼ cup vegetable oil
> 2 cups soy milk
> ½ tablespoon honey

Mix dry ingredients together. Then add the remaining ingredients and mix well. Preheat lightly oiled frying pan over medium heat. (An electric frying pan is excellent for pancakes.) Pour batter into frying pan and cook on both sides.
Makes 4 servings. 389 calories, 27 g fat, 147 mg sodium.
SERVING IDEA: Serve with fruit compote, p. 13.

Potato Pancakes

• PAMELA WILLIAMS

> 1 pound potatoes, peeled and sliced
> ½ teaspoon salt
> Vegetable oil spray
> 1 large onion, chopped
> 1 cup part-skim mozzarella cheese, shredded

Boil the potatoes in water with ½ teaspoon salt. Drain and mash. Spray skillet with vegetable oil spray and sauté the onion until soft. Add the onions to the potatoes and mix well. Add ½ cup of cheese and mix well. Shape the potatoes into eight balls. Divide the rest of the cheese into eight parts and push a portion of cheese into each ball. Flatten each ball to about ½ inch thick. Refrigerate for 1 hour.

Spray cookie sheet with vegetable spray and place the eight pancakes on it. Bake at 350° F for 20 minutes or until brown. Flip pancake over with spatula and brown other side, then serve.
Makes 4 servings. 219 calories, 10 g fat, 372 mg sodium.

Whole-Grain Waffles
• PAMELA AND ERMA WILLIAMS

2½ cups rolled oats
¾ cup cornmeal
1 teaspoon salt
⅓ cup nuts, blended in 1 cup water
¼ teaspoon nutmeg

Place all ingredients in a large bowl. Stir in 4 to 4½ cups hot water. Batter will be thin to make lighter waffles. Bake in hot waffle iron for 8 to 12 minutes. Do not peek until 8 minutes have passed. Serve with bananas, pecans, apples, raisins, and cinnamon, or other fruit toppings. Waffles can be frozen and later thawed in toaster oven.
Makes 8 servings. 214 calories, 4.5 g fat.

Strawberry Date Sauce
• RUTH DAVIS

2 cups fresh strawberries, sliced
½ cup orange juice frozen concentrate
1 cup chopped dates
½ cup water

Place ingredients in a microwavable bowl and cover with plastic wrap. Leave a small opening in cover to vent the steam. Microwave until hot. (Alternative method: place ingredients in pot, cover, and cook over medium heat until hot.) Serve over pancakes or French toast.
Makes 4 servings. 201 calories, 0.74 g fat, 4.5 mg sodium.

Peach Sauce
• JOCELYN M. PETERSON

4 ripe fresh peaches, washed, peeled, and sliced
⅓ cup molasses
1 cup water
1 teaspoon vanilla flavoring (optional)
1 teaspoon cinnamon (optional)
2 tablespoons cornstarch mixture (1 tablespoon cornstarch mixed with 1 tablespoon water)

Bring first five ingredients to a boil, then add cornstarch mixture. Continue boiling until sauce thickens. Cool. Serve over waffles or pancakes.
Makes 8 servings. 60 calories, trace fat, trace sodium.

Breakfast Shakes
• PAMELA WILLIAMS

5 ounces silken tofu, chilled and cubed
1 cup soy milk, chilled
1 cup fresh fruit, chopped and chilled in freezer for 1 hour
1 tablespoon honey
1 teaspoon vanilla extract
2 teaspoons soy protein powder (optional)

Combine all ingredients in a blender; blend until smooth. Serve in chilled glasses garnished with orange slices or mint sprigs. Various combinations can be added, such as 2 tablespoons peanut butter and 1 tablespoon carob powder, or 1 cup pineapple juice, 1 cup orange juice, and banana.
Makes 2 servings. 166 calories, 8 g fat, 101 mg sodium.

Breakfast

Scrambled Tofu
• PAMELA WILLIAMS

   2 tablespoons onion, chopped
   8 ounces firm tofu
   2 teaspoons dried basil
  ½ cup water
  ½ teaspoon McKay's Chicken Style Seasoning
  ¼ teaspoon turmeric

Spray medium saucepan with vegetable cooking spray. Sauté onions until tender. Add tofu and cook for an additional minute. Add basil, water, chicken-style seasoning, and turmeric, stirring to keep from sticking. Cook for an additional 3 minutes or until flavors are blended.
Makes 2 servings. 80 calories, 4 g fat, 142 mg sodium.

Scrambled Tofu With Mushrooms
• RUTH DAVIS

   1 pound tofu, crumbled
   2 teaspoons McKay's Chicken Style Seasoning
   1 small onion, minced
   1 cup mushrooms, sliced
   1 teaspoon garlic powder
   1 tablespoon soybean, olive, or corn oil

Crumble the tofu and add McKay's Chicken Style Seasoning in a mixing bowl. Sauté minced onion and sliced mushrooms in a skillet on medium heat. Add crumbled tofu mixture to onion and mushrooms; cover and cook for 5 minutes over low heat.
Makes 6 servings. 55 calories, 3.4 g fat, 43.4 mg sodium.
MENU SUGGESTION: Serve with rice, grits, or whole wheat toast.

Tofu Garden Scramble
• PAMELA AND ERMA WILLIAMS

   ½ cup onion, chopped
   ½ cup fresh mushrooms, chopped
   ¼ cup green and /or red bell pepper, chopped
   1 tablespoon tamari sauce
     Pam spray
   ½ teaspoon salt
   2 cups firm tofu, drained and crumbled
     Pinch of fresh garlic
     Dash of turmeric

Spray nonstick skillet with Pam. Sauté onion, bell pepper, mushrooms, and garlic. Add seasonings and let simmer several minutes. Add tofu, mixing until evenly distributed.
Makes 6 servings. 69 calories, 2 g fat.

Scrambled Tofu With Peppers
• JOCELYN M. PETERSON

   ½ cup chopped onions
   ½ cup chopped green peppers
   2 tablespoons olive oil
   1 pound tofu, rinsed and drained
   1 teaspoon turmeric
   1 teaspoon garlic powder
   1 teaspoon McKay's Chicken Style Seasoning
   1 teaspoon Mrs. Dash's Seasoning

Braise onions and green peppers in olive oil 2-5 minutes. Add tofu and seasonings. Simmer 10-15 minutes. Stir to keep from sticking. Serve warm.
Makes 12 servings. 200 calories, 6 g fat, 120 mg sodium.

Scrambled Tofu With Burger
• DONNA GREEN GOODMAN

   2 pounds firm tofu
   2 tablespoons olive oil
   ¼ cup green pepper, chopped
   ¼ cup red pepper, chopped
   ½ cup sweet onion, chopped
   1 clove garlic, chopped
   ½ cup vegan burger or sausage (optional)
   1 tablespoon McKay's Chicken Style Seasoning
   1 tablespoon Bragg Liquid Aminos (soy sauce substitute)
   1 teaspoon nutritional yeast flakes
   ¼ teaspoon turmeric

Rinse and drain tofu, then crumble or cut into strips. Heat oil in skillet; sauté vegetables. Add tofu and seasonings. Heat thoroughly and serve warm. (Sage and parsley are optional seasonings.)
Makes 8 servings. 65 calories, 5 g fat, 5 mg sodium

Breakfast Hash
• JOCELYN PETERSON

   3 medium-sized potatoes, cooked in skins, peeled
   2 tablespoons oil
   1 medium onion, diced
   2 breakfast patties, diced
   2 slices whole wheat bread, cubed
   1 teaspoon McKay's Chicken Style Seasonings
   3 tablespoons soy milk

Dice or shred cooked potatoes. Heat oil; sauté diced onion until clear but not brown. Add potatoes, breakfast patties, cubed bread, and seasonings. Stir. Sprinkle the soy milk over the mixture, cover, and simmer over low heat. Turn once. When lightly browned on both sides, serve on a warm plate.
Makes 4 servings. 120 calories, 3 g fat, 30 mg sodium.

Quick Hash Brown Breakfast Dish
• RUTH DAVIS

- 2 cups frozen hash brown potatoes
- 2 cups raw chopped mushrooms
- ½ cup diced onions
- 2 Worthington® Leanies®, diced

Place frozen hash brown potatoes in a microwave baking dish. Sprinkle chopped mushrooms and onions over the potatoes. Slice Leanies® and place over the above ingredients. Place plastic wrap over the baking dish, leaving a small open space on one corner. Microwave for 15 minutes. Remove and serve.
Makes 4 servings. 143 calories, 13 g fat, 243 mg sodium.
MENU SUGGESTION: Serve with Fruit Compote (p. 9) and orange juice.

Southern Scrapple
• PAMELA AND ERMA WILLIAMS

- 4 cups hot water
- ½ teaspoon salt
- 1 tablespoon garlic powder
- 1 tablespoon sage
- 2 cups yellow cornmeal
- 1 package Morningstar Farms® Breakfast Links, crumbled.

In a double boiler, combine water, salt, garlic powder, and sage. Heat mixture over hot water for 10 minutes. Add cornmeal gradually, stirring until smooth. Add links, stirring to distribute evenly. Cover and steam over hot water for 3 hours, adding water to bottom of double boiler as needed. Pour mixture into pan sprayed with nonstick vegetable spray. Chill until ready to use, unmold, cut into slices, and pan fry in nonstick pan as desired.
Makes 6 servings. 233 calories, 5.5 g fat, 400 mg sodium.

Philadelphia Scrapple, Vegetarian Style
• JOCELYN M. PETERSON

- 2 teaspoon olive oil
- 2 teaspoons McKay's Beef Style Seasoning
- ½ teaspoon sage
- 1 quart water
- 1½ cups cornmeal
- 2 cups cold water
- 2 cups seasoned shredded gluten or other meat analog

Place first four ingredients in top of a double boiler and heat over direct heat. Mix cornmeal with two cups of water, stir into boiling stock. Cook, stirring until thick. Add shredded gluten. Cook 1 hour over boiling water in double boiler. Pour into an oiled loaf pan. Chill several hours. Unmold and slice in ¾-inch slices. Lay slices on an oiled cookie sheet, brush with oil, and bake or broil until heated thoroughly and delicately browned. For crispness, dust with flour and brown in a small amount of oil over low heat. Serve hot with honey, applesauce, or other topping.
Makes 6 servings. 300 calories, 8 g fat, 250 mg sodium.

Spanish Sausage
• PAMELA AND ERMA WILLIAMS

- ½ pound Worthington® Prosage® Links, thawed (or 1 package Morningstar Farms® Breakfast Links)
- ½ cup green pepper, diced
- ½ cup onion, diced
- 4 ounces tomato sauce
- 2 tablespoons water

Slice links into small chunks. Brown pieces in nonstick skillet sprayed with nonstick spray. Sauté green pepper and onion. (Do not brown.) Add links to vegetables, add tomato sauce and water. Simmer covered for 5 minutes. Uncover and simmer until liquid is absorbed.
Makes 4 servings. 179 calories, 6 g fat.

Breakfast Quiche
• BARBARA FRAZIER

- 2 cups cooked Goya coarse whole-grain cornmeal (use as grits)
- 2 teaspoons Spike seasoning
  Olive oil cooking spray
- 1 pound firm low-fat tofu
- ½ package frozen stir-fry peppers and onions
- 2 teaspoons turmeric
- 8 ounces fat-free Soya Kaas cheddar-style cheese, grated
- 2 teaspoons Fakin' Bacon Bits

Cook Goya cornmeal (grits) in covered saucepan with 2 cups water and 1 teaspoon Spike seasoning. Spoon grits evenly in 7-inch glass pie pan and set aside on stove. Place skillet on stove and spray generously with cooking spray. Rinse tofu with water. Squeeze dry while crumbling in large wad of paper towels. Drop tofu into skillet. Crumble with fork as needed to resemble scrambled eggs. Add vegetables, turmeric, and remaining Spike. Stir fry mixture until seasonings are adequately blended and tofu is heated through. Add grated cheese and cover until cheese melts. Sprinkle with Fakin' Bacon Bits. Spoon mixture into grits "pie shell." Slice in wedges and serve.

Makes 8 servings. 157 calories, 2 g fat, 9 g protein, 357 mg sodium.

Breakfast Patties
• PAMELA AND ERMA WILLIAMS

- 1 cup cooked oatmeal
- ⅓ cup cashew butter
- 1 medium onion, chopped
- 1 cup bread crumbs
- ½ cup chopped mushrooms
- 2 eggs (or egg substitute equivalent)
- 2 tablespoons soy milk
- ½ teaspoon sage
  Garlic powder to taste
  Salt to taste
- 1 can cream of mushroom soup

Combine ingredients and drop as patties in skillet sprayed with nonstick spray. When done, place patties in a casserole, cover with diluted cream of mushroom soup, and bake at 375° F until bubbly.

Makes 6 servings. 188 calories, 7 g fat.

Breakfast is the first chance the body has to refuel its glucose levels, also known as blood sugar, after eight to 12 hours without a meal or snack. Glucose is essential for the brain and is the main energy source. Blood glucose also helps fuel the muscles needed for physical activity throughout the day.

Breads and

When people hear "whole grains," they often think of whole wheat. That one is great, but there are many more grains to choose from. Several may even have more nutrients than whole wheat. Examples of other grains include oats, barley, millet, rye, brown rice, corn (maize), buckwheat, and amaranth. Here is a collection of breads and muffins that will help keep you in good health.

Applesauce Nut Bread
• DONNA A. SMITH

  1 egg (or egg substitute equivalent), slightly beaten
  1 cup unsweetened applesauce
  ½ cup vegetable oil
  ½ cup brown sugar
  1 cup raisins
  ⅓ cup chopped walnuts
 1¾ cups flour
  2 teaspoons baking powder
  ½ teaspoon salt
 1½ teaspoon cinnamon
  ½ teaspoon allspice

Preheat oven to 350° F. Combine first six ingredients and mix well. Sift flour, baking powder, salt, and spices together. Mix into applesauce mixture. Pour into 9" x 5" bread pan sprayed with vegetable pan spray. Bake for 1 hour. Cool 10 minutes before removing from pan.

Makes 16 slices. 219 calories, 10 g fat, 144 mg sodium.

Banana Bread
• JOHNETTE M. FRAZIER

  2 cups unbleached flour
  ⅓ cup canola oil
  1 teaspoon baking soda
  1 cup sugar or ¾ cup honey
  2 eggs (or egg substitute equivalent)
  2 teaspoons salt
  ¾ cup sugar
  2 teaspoons vanilla
  4 ripe bananas, mashed

Mix all ingredients well. Pour into loaf pan sprayed with Pam. Bake at 350°F for approximately 50 minutes.

Makes 12 servings. 229 calories, 8 g fat, 211 mg sodium.

Egg Replacements In Desserts and Sweet, Baked Goods: Try substituting one banana or ¼ cup applesauce for each egg called for in a recipe for sweet, baked desserts. These will add some flavor to the recipe, so make sure bananas or apples are compatible with the other flavors in the dessert.

www.vegcooking.com

Egg Replacement Options
Tasty Tidbit:

• 1 egg = 2 Tbsp. potato starch
• 1 egg = ¼ cup mashed potatoes
• 1 egg = ¼ cup canned pumpkin or squash
• 1 egg = ¼ cup puréed prunes
• 1 egg = 2 Tbsp. water + 1 Tbsp. oil + 2 tsp. baking powder
• 1 egg = 1 Tbsp. ground flax seed simmered in 3 Tbsp. water
• 1 egg white = 1 Tbsp. plain agar powder dissolved in 1 Tbsp. water, whipped, chilled, and whipped again

Banana/Mango Bread
• JOHNETTA FRAZIER

    1 cup soy margarine
    3 eggs (or egg substitute equivalent)
    1 cup packed brown sugar or ⅞ cup honey
    3 cups self-rising flour
    ½ teaspoon salt
    ¼ teaspoon nutmeg
    1 teaspoon cinnamon
    1 mango, peeled and pureed
    2 large ripe bananas, mashed
    ¾ cup chopped walnuts
    1 cup raisins

Cream margarine, eggs, and sugar together. Mix dry ingredients together in a separate bowl. In a third bowl, combine mango and bananas. Combine flour and banana mixture alternately with egg mixture. Add nuts and raisins. Pour into two loaf pans sprayed with Pam. Bake at 350° F for 55 minutes.
Makes 20 servings. 273 calories, 14 g fat, 385 mg sodium.

Pecan Raisin Bread
• PAMELA AND ERMA WILLIAMS

    3 cups warm water
    2 tablespoons honey
    5 tablespoons yeast
    ¼ cup brown sugar
    2 tablespoons oil
    1½ cups oatmeal
    2 cups whole wheat flour
    3 cups soybean puree
      (1 cup soybeans blended with 2 cups water)
    ½ cup wheat germ
    1 tablespoon salt
    ½ cup raisins
    1 cup pecans, chopped

Mix the first three ingredients and let rise for 10 minutes. Stir in next seven ingredients and let rise for a half hour. Blend in pecans and raisins. Knead well with ½ cup whole wheat flour to make a soft

dough. Let rise until double in size. Put in pans and let rise again. Bake at 375° F for 10 minutes. Then bake at 350° F for 50 minutes.
Makes 16 servings. 208 calories, 6.4 g fat.

Coconut Bread
• JOHNETTA FRAZIER

    1 tablespoon yeast
    1 cup sugar
    2½ cups unbleached flour
    1½ cups grated coconut
    ¼ teaspoon salt
    3 tablespoons soy margarine
    ¾ cup raisins or other dried fruit

Sprinkle yeast in bowl with one cup warm water. Add one tablespoon sugar and two tablespoons of flour. Stir well and allow to rise. Mix coconut, sugar, salt, and margarine in separate bowl. Add yeast mixture, flour, and dried fruit. Mix well. Grease another bowl with margarine. Place dough in greased bowl. Cover bowl with towel and allow dough to rise until double in size. Knead dough again and then divide in half. Place each half in a greased loaf pan. Cover each pan with a towel and allow the dough to rise again. Bake bread in 350° F oven for 30 minutes. Remove bread from oven and brush top of bread with a mixture of honey and soy margarine.
Makes 20 servings. 149 calories, 4 g fat, 44 mg sodium.

Gingerbread
• JOHNETTA FRAZIER

    1 cup unbleached flour
    ¾ teaspoon ground ginger
    ¾ teaspoon cinnamon
    ⅓ teaspoon baking powder
    ½ cup soy margarine
    ¼ cup brown sugar
    2 eggs (or egg substitute equivalent)
    ½ cup molasses
    ½ cup boiling water

Mix together dry ingredients. Cream margarine and brown sugar. Add eggs and molasses to brown sugar mixture. Add dry ingredients and boiling water alternately to cream mixture. Pour into greased and floured 9-inch square pan. Bake at 350° F for 30 minutes.
Makes 8 servings. 278 calories, 13 g fat, 223 mg sodium.

Banana Date Nut Muffins

• RUTH DAVIS

- 4-5 bananas, mashed
- 2 tablespoons vegetable oil (soybean)
- 1 cup water
- 2 cups whole wheat flour
- 2½ teaspoons baking powder
- ½ cup chopped walnuts
- 1 cup chopped dates

Preheat oven to 425° F. Grease the bottom of a muffin pan or use paper baking cups. In a mixing bowl, blend the mashed bananas, vegetable oil, and water. Add flour, baking powder, nuts, and dates to the liquid mixture. Stir until dry ingredients are moistened (don't over mix). Fill muffin cups about two-thirds full and bake for 15-20 minutes or until golden brown. Remove from oven; cool for 5 minutes in the pan before removing.
Makes 16 servings. 125 calories, 0.5 g fat, 1.13 mg sodium.

Raisin Muffins

• PAMELA AND ERMA WILLIAMS

- 2 tablespoons yeast
- ½ cup lukewarm water
- 1½ cups raisins
- 2 teaspoons salt
- 5½ cups hot water
- 3 cups whole wheat flour
- 2 cups oatmeal
- ½ cup bran

Soften yeast in lukewarm water. Mix raisins, salt, and hot water. Add flour, bran, and oatmeal. When cool, add yeast. Stir. Fill muffin cups half full. Let rise until double in size. Bake at 350°F for 20 minutes. (You may have to add a little water to get the right consistency.) Variations: For raisins substitute 1½ cups dates or apricots, or 1 cup chopped and dried cranberries and 2 tablespoons orange peel.
Makes 16 servings. 162 calories, 2.5 g fat.

Cinnamon Banana Muffins

• JOHNETTA FRAZIER

- 2 cups flour
- 2 teaspoons baking powder
- ½ teaspoon salt
- ½ teaspoon cinnamon
- 2 ripe bananas
- ¼ cup soy milk
- ½ cup soy margarine
- ½ cup honey
- 2 eggs (or egg substitute equivalent)
- 1 teaspoon vanilla

Combine dry ingredients. Combine bananas and milk in separate bowl. Cream margarine and honey and then add remaining ingredients to creamed mixture. Add banana mixture alternately with flour mixture. Fill muffin tins ⅔ full. Bake at 375° F for 25 to 30 minutes.
Makes 12 servings. 204 calories, 9 g fat, 172 mg sodium.

Skillet Corn Bread
• JOCELYN M. PETERSON

    1 cup yellow cornmeal
    ¼ cup bread flour
    1 cup boiling water
    2 tablespoons olive oil
    ½ cup Scramblers egg substitute
    1 tablespoon honey
    ¼ cup almond nut milk

Mix dry ingredients in a large bowl. Pour boiling water over them and blend well, using more or less water as needed to make a medium batter. Warm oil in skillet and stir into batter. Mix Scramblers with honey and soy milk. Fold gently into batter to preserve air in batter. (This is what makes the cornbread light.) Pour batter into a hot oiled skillet. Have lid warm also. Cover and place over low to medium heat. Bake until set, about 15 minutes. Uncover, loosen around edges with knife or spatula, and turn corn bread over. Bake about 10 minutes longer, uncovered, to brown top crust (now on bottom). If you wish to bake this in the oven, do not cover. Bake at 350° F for 25 minutes or until done. (Test with toothpick.)
Makes 6 servings. 180 calories, 4 g fat, 60 mg sodium.

Soy-Corn Muffins
• PAT HUMPHREY

    2 cups soaked soybeans, drained
    2 cups water
    2 tablespoons honey
    2 tablespoons oil
    ¼ cup quick oatmeal
    1½ teaspoons salt, or to taste
    2 cups plain cornmeal

Blend first six ingredients at high setting until creamy. Pour batter into bowl and stir in cornmeal. Bake in muffin tin sprayed with vegetable spray at 375° F for about 45 minutes. (Baking time may vary according to the oven.)
Makes 18 muffins. 99 calories, 2.5 g fat, 261 mg

Southern-Style Corn Bread
• DONNA A. SMITH

    1 teaspoon dried minced onion
    1 15-ounce package corn bread mix
 1¼ cups water
    1 8¾-ounce can cream-style corn
  ⅛ teaspoon cayenne pepper
  ½ cup tofutti sour cream
    1 tablespoon all-purpose flour
    1 cup almond/rice shredded cheddar cheese

Place onion in 1 teaspoon water and let stand for 5 minutes. In medium mixing bowl combine corn bread mix, water, cream-style corn, and cayenne pepper. Spread mixture in greased 12" x 7½" x 2" baking dish. In a medium mixing bowl stir together sour cream and flour, add onion and ½ cup of the cheese, then lightly spoon over batter in pan. Bake at 350° F for 40 minutes, or until top is golden. Sprinkle top with remaining cheese.

Yield: 12 servings. 206 calories, 206, 2 g fat, 544 mg sodium.

Yeast Corn Bread
• JOCELYN M PETERSON

 2½ cups wheat flour
    1 tablespoon yeast
    1 tablespoon honey
 2½ cups warm water
    1 tablespoon olive oil
    2 cups cornmeal

Mix warm water, oil, and honey and add to dry ingredients and yeast. Stir just enough to moisten all ingredients. Lightly spread margarine into a prepared 9" x 13" x ¾" baking pan and add mixture. Let rise, then bake at 350° F for 45 minutes or until done. Let cool. (This is best cooked the day before needed and reheated.)

Makes 12 servings. 85 calories, trace fat, less than 5 mg sodium.

Soups and

O ften *soup du jour,* or soup of the day, is served as an appetizer. Today's families are choosing soups as the main entree. That's because soups not only come in many varieties, but they add much nutritional value. With a food processor and some preparation, making healthy soups can be hassle-free—and you can control the sodium content. Canned soups contain as much as 1,000 milligrams of sodium per serving. That is almost half the recommended amount for an entire day. *Tip du jour:* Halt the salt and treat your family to these wholesome, creative soups.

Hearty Soup
• DONNA A. SMITH

    1 onion, chopped
    1 green pepper, chopped
    1 garlic clove, minced
    1 tablespoon margarine or vegetable oil
    1 package tofu, drained and cubed
    1 large tomato, chopped
    1 cup George Washington Rich Brown Seasoning broth
    1 8-ounce can low-sodium tomato sauce
    1 15-ounce can vegetarian beans
    1 cup water
      Salt and cayenne pepper to taste

In a large skillet, sauté onion, green pepper, and garlic cloves in margarine or vegetable oil. Add tofu, tomato, broth, and seasonings. Simmer 10 minutes. In a large pot, add sautéed mixture to remaining ingredients and heat until hot.
Makes 6 servings. 121 calories, 2 g fat, 576 mg sodium.

Buttermilk-Potato Soup
• DONNA A. SMITH

    ¾ cup soy flour or all-purpose flour
    1 tablespoon margarine
    4 cups soy milk
    1 cup nondairy sour cream
    3 slices veggie provolone/Swiss cheese, shredded
    3 large potatoes, cooked and peeled
    1 large cucumber, peeled and diced
    3 tablespoons fresh chives, minced
    1 tablespoon lemon juice
    1 teaspoon thyme
    1 teaspoon tarragon leaves
      Salt and cayenne pepper to taste
      Fresh parsley
      Seasoned croutons

In a large skillet, make a white sauce by cooking flour and margarine, then slowing adding 2 cups soy milk, stirring constantly until the sauce thickens. Add sour cream and shredded cheese. Puree potatoes in a food processor or blender while adding a little milk. In a large pot, add white sauce, pureed potatoes, remaining ingredients and seasonings. Garnish with fresh parsley and seasoned croutons.
Makes 8 servings. 177 calories, 8 g fat, 234 mg sodium.

Is your soup too salty tasting? Then place a raw potato in the pot and simmer with the soup for about 15 minutes. Remove it before serving. Not only does it absorb the extra salt, but it also absorbs all that flavor and becomes a great treat for the cook!

www.easy-appetizer-recipes.com

Cream of Potato Soup
• PAT HUMPHREY

    2 medium onions, finely chopped
    8 sticks of celery
  ½ cup fresh parsley
    5 cups water
    5 potatoes, cubed
    2 teaspoons salt
    1 teaspoon sweet basil
  ½ teaspoon thyme
  ¼ teaspoon oregano
  ½ cup raw cashews
    1 cup water

Steam onions, celery, and parsley in ½ cup water 5 to 8 minutes. Add remaining ingredients and boil until potatoes are tender. Blend cashews and 1 cup water. Add to soup and simmer.
Makes 20 servings (½ cup each). 38 calories, 1.7 g fat, 236 mg sodium.

Cream of Pea Soup
• DONNA A. SMITH

    1 cup carrots, shredded
    1 cup dried split peas
    1 cup McKay's Chicken Style Seasoning broth (make broth according to directions)
    1 cup onions, chopped
    1 tablespoon margarine
    2 tablespoons soy flour or all-purpose flour
    1 cup soy milk
      Salt and cayenne pepper to taste

Combine carrots, peas, chicken broth, and onions in saucepan; bring to boil, reduce heat, and simmer until peas are tender. Pour vegetable mixture into blender and blend until smooth. In the same saucepan, melt margarine and stir in flour; add milk gradually, stirring until smooth. Cook and stir until mixture thickens and bubbles. Add vegetable puree and stir until well blended; season to taste.
Makes 4 servings. 148 calories, 4 g fat, 505 mg sodium.

Cream of Chicken Soup With Herbs
• DONNA A. SMITH

    1 onion, chopped
    1 stalk celery, chopped
 1-2 tablespoons margarine
  ¾ cup soy flour or all-purpose flour
    1 12-ounce container of nondairy sour cream
    2 cups soy milk
    1 12.5-ounce can FriChik (low fat), cubed
    3 bay leaves
    1 tablespoon fresh chives, minced
    1 teaspoon thyme
    1 teaspoon turmeric
    1 cup water
      Salt and cayenne pepper to taste
      Sesame seeds
      Fresh parsley

In a large skillet, sauté onion and celery in margarine until tender. Gradually blend flour, sour cream, and milk, stirring constantly. Add cubed chicken to sauce, and then add bay leaves and seasonings. Simmer 10 minutes. Transfer to a large pot and add 1 cup water and heat until hot. Sprinkle with sesame seeds and fresh parsley.
Makes 6 servings. 153 calories, 0 g fat, 253 mg sodium.

Chicken Gumbo
• DONNA A. SMITH

    1 tablespoon vegetable oil
    1 onion, chopped
    1 tablespoon soy flour or all-purpose flour
    1 cup soy milk
    1 12.5 ounce can FriChik, diced (low fat), reserve broth
    2 tomatoes, diced
    2 cups frozen breaded okra, thawed
    1 cup fresh corn
    2 cups water

In a large skillet, sauté onion in oil; add flour, then slowly add milk and broth from chicken. Add chicken, tomatoes, okra, and seasonings. Simmer

until well seasoned. Transfer to a large pot and add corn and water. Cook until corn is done.
Makes 8 servings. 135 calories, 0 g fat, 176 mg sodium.

Split-Pea Chowder
• PAT HUMPHREY

   1 onion, chopped
   1 tomato, wedged
   2 tablespoons olive oil
   4 cups water
   ½ pound split peas
   2 teaspoons salt
   1 tablespoon garlic powder
   ½ teaspoon thyme
   ½ teaspoon basil

Sauté onion and tomato in olive oil. Add water and split peas. Bring to a boil, add seasonings, and cook over low heat for 1½ hours. Add water as necessary.
Makes 8 servings. 131 calories, 4 g fat, 514 mg sodium.

Green Pea Stew
• PAMELA WILLIAMS

   1 clove garlic, minced
   1 tablespoon oil
   1 teaspoon paprika
   2 10-ounce packages Worthington Stakelets, cut into cubes
   1 large onion, minced
   1 tablespoon soy flour
  1½ cups hot water
   ½ teaspoon salt
   Dash of cayenne pepper
  1½ cups green peas, fresh or frozen
   2 eggs (or egg substitute equivalent), beaten
   ¼ cup fresh parsley, chopped

In a large saucepan over medium heat, sauté garlic in oil until garlic turns brown. Remove garlic. Stir in paprika. Add cubes of Stakelets and onions and stir until onions are soft. Add flour and cook for 2

minutes, stirring constantly. Add hot water, salt, and pepper. Cover and cook for 1 hour on low heat. Add peas and simmer 15 minutes. Remove peas and Stakelets from the pan. Stir in eggs and parsley, constantly stirring until sauce thickens slightly. Do not let it boil or it will curdle. Pour the sauce over the Stakelets and peas. Serve with mashed potatoes or root vegetable.
Makes 6 servings. 197 calories, 9 g fat, 541 mg sodium.

Black-Eyed Pea Soup
• DONNA A. SMITH

   1 16-ounce package dried black-eyed peas
   1 onion
   4 bay leaves
   1 garlic clove
   3 tablespoons margarine
   Salt and cayenne pepper to taste

In a large pot, prepare black-eyed peas according to directions on package. Put onion, bay leaves, garlic, clove, and margarine in pot. Season with salt and cayenne pepper to taste. Simmer.
Makes 8 servings. 122 calories, 5 g fat, 56 mg sodium.

Herb Lentil Soup
• JOCELYN M. PETERSON

    2 cups dried lentils
    2 carrots, finely chopped
    2 quarts water
    1 large onion, chopped
    2 stalks celery, chopped
    2 teaspoons garlic powder
    2 bay leaves
    1 teaspoon Mrs. Dash seasoning (optional)
    2 tablespoons margarine
    ½ cup chopped parsley

Cook all ingredients except margarine and parsley until lentils are done (approximately 1 hour). Add margarine, and parsley, and serve with plain croutons.
Makes 6 servings. 150 calories, 2 g fat, 10 mg sodium.

Lentil Stew
• DONNA A. SMITH

    1 pound dried lentils
    1 onion, minced
  4-5 stalks celery, chopped
    1 tablespoon vegetable oil
  4-5 bay leaves
    1 teaspoon curry powder
    1 cup parsley, chopped
    1 teaspoon cumin
    1 teaspoon coriander
       Salt and cayenne pepper to taste

In a large pot, prepare lentils according to directions. Sauté onion and celery in hot oiled skillet. Add onion, celery, bay leaves, and seasonings to large pot. Simmer until lentils are well seasoned.
Makes 6 servings. 207 calories, 3 g fat, 121 mg sodium.

North African Lentil Soup (Africa)
• ERMA WILLIAMS

    1 cup lentils, uncooked
    6 cups cold water
    1 tablespoon olive oil
    1 onion, diced
       Salt
       Cayenne pepper
    1 carrot, diced
    1 celery stalk, diced
    1 red bell pepper, diced
    1 8-ounce can chopped tomatoes
    ½ teaspoon ground cumin
    1 teaspoon ground coriander
    ⅛ teaspoon turmeric
    4 garlic cloves, minced
    2 tablespoons chopped cilantro

Rinse lentils and place them in 6 cups of cold water in a soup pot. Boil, reduce heat, and simmer uncovered for 20 minutes. Meanwhile, heat the olive oil in a sauté pan and add the onion, salt, and very small amount of cayenne pepper. Cook over medium heat until onions are soft. Then add vegetables and the rest of the spices. Cook for 5 minutes. Stir in garlic and cook for 2 minutes. Add this mixture to the lentils. Cover and cook for 30 minutes. Serve and garnish with cilantro.
Makes 8 servings. 117 calories, 3 g fat.
COOK'S HINT: Vegetable spray can be substituted for the olive oil. If necessary, add 1 to 2 teaspoons water to keep food from sticking.

Egyptian Stew
• PAT HUMPHREY

    2 tablespoons oil
    1 cup onion, sliced
    ½ cup green pepper, sliced
    2 cups corn kernels
    2 cups lima beans, cooked
    ⅓ cup tomatoes, fresh or canned
    2 cups zucchini, sliced
    ½ cup parsley, chopped

Sauté onions and green pepper in oil. Add corn and lima beans and cook on low heat for 15 minutes. Add tomatoes and zucchini and cook an additional 15 to 20 minutes. Add parsley just before serving. Serve in bowls.
Makes 8 servings. 242 calories, 4 g fat, 29 mg sodium.

Peanut Soup
• ERMA WILLIAMS

1 10-ounce jar dry roasted peanuts, pureed
2 cups tofu, soy or nonfat milk
2 cups water
2 teaspoons McKay's Chicken Style Seasoning
2 teaspoons minced chives
2 garlic cloves, minced
1 tablespoon grated carrots

Place all ingredients in a large saucepan, and heat, stirring every 15 to 20 minutes. Serve hot. (This soup should be served in small quantities because of the high fat content of the peanuts.)
Makes 8 servings. 183 calories, 13 g fat.

Pinto Bean Soup
• DONNA A. SMITH

2 cups dried pinto beans
1 onion, chopped
3 tablespoons flour
1-2 tablespoons margarine
2 cups milk
1 teaspoon thyme
1 teaspoon Old Hickory Smoke Salt
1 teaspoon Perc Garden Seasoning or Mrs. Dash
1 teaspoon rosemary leaves
1 cup cooked, diced potatoes
2-3 tablespoons imitation bacon bits
Salt and cayenne pepper to taste

In a large pot, cook beans according to directions. In a separate skillet make grams by sautéing onions and browning flour in margarine. Slowly add one cup of milk and seasoning. Add gravy, potatoes, imitation bacon bits, and additional cup of milk to cooked beans and heat until hot.
Makes 6 servings. 153 calories, 2 g fat, 256 mg sodium.

Fast 'n' Easy Bean Soup
• PAMELA AND ERMA WILLIAMS

1 tablespoon olive oil
1 medium onion, chopped
2 cloves garlic, minced
1 15½-ounce can kidney beans, drained
1 15½-ounce can pinto beans, drained
1 cup quick-cooking brown rice
1 package frozen chopped spinach
1 package frozen corn
3 cups water
2 cups tomato puree
1 green bell pepper, chopped
1 teaspoon McKay's Chicken Style Seasoning
2 teaspoons basil
1 teaspoon dried oregano
Croutons

Heat oil in a large saucepan over medium heat. Add onions and garlic. Cook until onions are translucent. Add all ingredients except croutons and bring to a boil. Reduce heat, cover, and simmer for 10 minutes or until rice is cooked. Spoon into serving bowls and top with croutons. Serve with garlic bread.
Makes 6 servings. 267 calories, 5 g fat.

Chickpea Soup (Morocco)
• PAMELA A. WILLIAMS

       2 medium carrots, cut into thin strips
       3 garlic cloves, chopped
       1 large onion, chopped
       3 cups water
       3 teaspoons McKay's Chicken Style
         Seasoning
   1½ cups chickpeas, drained
       2 tablespoons tahini
       2 tablespoons fresh lemon juice
       2 tablespoons chopped parsley
       ½ teaspoon ground cumin
       ½ teaspoon thyme
       ¼ teaspoon turmeric
         paprika
         green onions, chopped

Spray a medium saucepan with vegetable oil and
sauté carrots, garlic, and onion; cook until tender and
set aside. Mix water and chicken seasoning. In food
processor puree chickpeas, one cup of chicken broth,
tahini, and lemon juice. Add remaining ingredients.
Cover and cook until heated thoroughly. Serve in
soup bowls; garnish with paprika and green onions.
Makes 4 servings. 334 calories, 5 g fat, 686 mg sodium.

White Bean Chowder
• ERMA WILLIAMS

       1 cup dried navy beans
       ¾ cup onions, chopped
       2 potatoes, cubed
       2 carrots, diced
       2 stalks celery, diced
       1 cup tomatoes, pureed
       1 tablespoon vegetarian bacon bits
       2 cups tofu, soy or nonfat milk
       1 teaspoon salt
       2 tablespoons parsley, chopped

Soak the beans in 4 cups of water overnight and
drain. Add 3 cups fresh water, boil, and cook for 30
minutes over low heat. Add vegetables and
vegetarian bacon bits and cook for 35 minutes

more. Puree 3 cups of the bean mixture in a blender
or food processor and return to the rest of the soup.
Add milk, salt, and parsley. Stir. Let simmer for 5
minutes.
Makes 6 servings. 170 calories, 0.5 g fat.

Vegetable Kidney Bean Soup
• CHRISTINA FLEMING GABRIEL

       2 cups water
       1 16-ounce package frozen stir fry
         vegetables, thawed
   1½ cups cooked brown rice
       ½ cup tomato paste
       ½ teaspoon each: garlic powder, basil,
         oregano, and crushed red pepper
   1½ cups canned kidney beans

Place water and thawed vegetables in a medium
size pot. Bring to a boil over high heat. Add cooked
rice, tomato paste, seasonings, and kidney beans.
Reduce heat and simmer until vegetables are
cooked thoroughly.
Makes 6 servings. 176 calories, 4.1 g fat,
186 mg sodium.

Lima Bean Chowder
• PAT HUMPHREY

       3 tablespoons onion, chopped
       2 medium potatoes, diced
       1 tablespoon oil
       1 cup water
       1 package frozen lima beans
       1 16-ounce can stewed tomatoes
       3 cups nut milk (¾ cups nuts, 1 cup water)
       3 tablespoons unbleached flour
       ½ teaspoon celery salt
       ¼ teaspoon paprika
   1½ teaspoons McKay's Chicken Style
         Seasoning

In deep skillet, sauté onion and potatoes in oil 2 to 3
minutes. Add ½ cup water, then cover and steam
about 10 minutes. Add remaining water and lima

beans. Cover and cook until limas are almost done. Add tomatoes. Blend nuts and water to make nut milk. Add flour and seasonings to blender and mix thoroughly. Add nut milk/seasoning mixture to lima beans and simmer on medium high heat, stirring constantly, until thickened. Serve hot.

Makes 8 servings. 196 calories, 9.3 g fat, 308 mg sodium.

All Beans in the Pot
• CHRISTINA FLEMING GABRIEL

 1 cup lentils, dry
 1 10-ounce package frozen black-eyed peas, thawed (may substitute any of your favorite beans)
 1 cup carrots, diced
 1 cup potatoes, diced
 1 onion, chopped
 1 6-ounce can tomato paste
 ½ teaspoon each: garlic powder, basil, oregano, and crushed red pepper
 salt (optional)

Cook beans in a large pot according to package directions. Just before the beans are completely done add carrots, potatoes, onions, and tomato paste. Simmer until vegetables are tender and beans are done. Add seasonings to achieve desired taste.

Makes 6 servings. 143 calories, 0.38 g fat, 53 mg sodium.

Soybean Harvest Soup
• PAMELA WILLIAMS

 10 sun-dried tomatoes (not packed in oil)
 1 cup boiling water
 3 large onions, chopped
 3 cloves garlic, chopped
 1 green bell pepper, chopped
 3 carrots, grated
 1 small potato, grated
 2 tablespoons olive oil
 1 bay leaf
 1 teaspoon ground cumin
 1 teaspoon fresh oregano
 1 teaspoon fresh thyme
 6 cups cooked soybeans
 2 cups water
 Salt to taste
 Fresh parsley, chopped

In a small bowl, cover the sun-dried tomatoes with the boiling water and set aside. In a soup pot, sauté the onions, garlic, bell pepper, carrots, and potatoes in olive oil for 5 minutes, stirring frequently. Add the bay leaf, cumin, oregano, and thyme. Stir until blended. Add soybeans and stir in about 2 cups of water or enough to make a thick soup. Cook for 30 minutes. Drain and chop the softened sun-dried tomatoes. Add the tomatoes to the soup and salt to taste; cook soup for 10 minutes longer. Serve hot with fresh parsley garnish.

Yield: 6 servings. 382 calories, 16 g fat, 33 mg sodium.

Gazpacho (Italy)
• ERMA WILLIAMS

- 5 pounds red tomatoes, blanched and peeled
- 1 medium cucumber, peeled and sliced (seed removed)
- ½ medium red onion, diced
- 2 tablespoons green bell pepper, diced
- 2 tablespoons lime juice
- 1 teaspoon McKay's Beef Style Seasoning
  Salt
  Cilantro, chopped

Cut peeled tomatoes in half. Press tomatoes through a strainer and remove seeds. Save the juice. Puree half of the tomatoes and coarsely chop the rest. Combine tomatoes, cucumber, onion, bell pepper, lime juice, beef-style seasoning, and salt to taste. Chill for at least 1 hour. Pour into serving bowls and garnish with cilantro. If too acidic, add a pinch of sugar.
Makes 8 servings. 21 calories, 0 g fat.

Miso Soup (Orient)
• PAMELA WILLIAMS

- 3 cloves garlic, crushed
- ¼ cup onions, thinly sliced
- 1 teaspoon fresh ginger, grated
- 1 cup carrots, sliced
- 1 cup bok choy or Chinese cabbage, shredded
- 1 cup mushrooms, sliced
- 2 tablespoon miso
- 4 cups water
- 8 ounces firm tofu, drained and cubed

Spray a medium soup pot with vegetable cooking spray and place over medium heat. Add garlic and onions; sauté for 1 minute. Add ginger, carrots, bok choy, and mushroom. Cook and stir for 2 minutes. Dissolve miso into 2 tablespoons water and add tofu. Heat for an additional 5-10 minutes until hot. Serve.

Tomato and Rice Soup
• DONNA A. SMITH

- 1 8-ounce can tomato sauce
- 3 cups brown rice, cooked
- 1 cup McKay's Chicken Style Seasoning broth
- 1 large tomato, chopped
- 1 teaspoon oregano
- 1 teaspoon sweet basil
- 1 teaspoon thyme
- 2-3 bay leaves
  Salt and cayenne pepper to taste

In a large pot, mix all ingredients and seasonings. Cook 20-30 minutes. Garnish with fresh parsley, shredded veggie cheese, graham crackers, or wheat thins.
Makes 5 servings. 137 calories, 0 g fat, 359 mg sodium.

Corn and Potato Chowder
• DONNA A. SMITH

- ⅛ cup vegetable stock (p. 38)
- 2 onions, chopped
- 2 garlic cloves, crushed
- 2 medium potatoes, chopped
- 2 stalks of celery, sliced
- 1 green bell pepper, sliced
- 1 tablespoon Braggs Liquid Aminos
- 2½ cups vegetable stock
- ½ cups soy or nut milk
- 1 cup fresh or frozen cooked lima beans
- 1 cup fresh or canned kernel corn
- ½ teaspoon sage or herb of choice
- 2 tablespoons lignin-rich flaxseed oil
- 4 tablespoons fresh, chopped parsley

Sauté the first seven ingredients in a saucepan for 10 minutes. Add stock and bring to a boil. Reduce heat and simmer for about 15 minutes. Add the milk, beans, corn, and sage. Continue to simmer for five-seven minutes. Stir in the flaxseed oil just before spooning into individual bowls. Sprinkle one tablespoon parsley over each serving. Makes 4 servings. 290 calories, 10 g fat, 130 mg sodium.

Lentil and Spinach Soup
• JUANITA ALEXANDER

  5 cups water
1½ cups raw lentils
  ½ teaspoon sea salt
  2 tablespoons water
  2 carrots, sliced
  1 onion, chopped
  3 garlic cloves, finely chopped
  4 cups vegetable stock (p. 38) or water
  3 cups water
  ⅛ teaspoon ground coriander seed
  ⅛ teaspoon cayenne
1½ teaspoons cumin
  2 tablespoons finely chopped fresh coriander
  ½ pound fresh spinach leaves, chopped
  2 tablespoons lignin-rich flaxseed oil

In a large stockpot, bring the water to a boil, add the lentils, and simmer uncovered for approximately 1 hour (until tender). Rinse, drain, and return the lentils to the stockpot and set aside. In a pan, sauté the carrots for 10 minutes; add the onions and garlic and cook until tender. In the stockpot add stock, water, ground coriander, cayenne, cumin, and spinach. Simmer uncovered for 15 minutes. Stir in fresh coriander leaves and flaxseed oil just before serving.
Makes 8 servings. 180 calories, 4 g fat, 180 mg sodium.

Zucchini Bisque
• JUANITA ALEXANDER

  2 tablespoons vegetable stock or water
  1 medium onion, chopped
1½ pounds sliced zucchini
2½ cups vegetable stock or water

  2 tablespoons nutritional yeast
  ⅛ teaspoon cayenne (optional)
  1 tablespoon Braggs Liquid Aminos
  ½ pound tofu
  4 tablespoons vegetable stock or water
  2 tablespoons lignin-rich flaxseed oil

Sauté the first three ingredients. Add the next four ingredients and simmer for 15 minutes. Remove from the heat and let cool approximately 5 minutes. Blend the tofu and four tablespoons of stock until smooth. Stir the tofu into the cooled vegetables, adjust seasonings if water was substituted for the stock, and heat gently. *Do not bring to a boil.* Stir in the flaxseed oil just before serving.
Makes 4 servings. 210 calories, 13 g fat, 60 mg sodium.

Cream of Tomato Soup
• JUANITA ALEXANDER

- ½ cup raw rinsed cashews
- 1½ cups well-cooked brown rice
- 2 cups Vegetable Stock (p. 38)
- 3 cups fresh or canned tomatoes
- ¼ cup honey or white grape juice concentrate
- ½ teaspoon sea salt
- 1½ teaspoons Emes chicken-flavored seasoning
- ¼ teaspoon savory
- ¼ teaspoon dill weed
- 2 cups Vegetable Stock (p. 38)
- 2 tablespoons nutritional yeast
- 2 tablespoons lignin-rich flaxseed oil

Combine the cashews and rice and blend in two batches (one cup of stock per batch) until smooth. Place in a stockpot. Blend the tomatoes until smooth. Add to the rice and cashew mixture. Stir in the next seven ingredients. Adjust the seasonings. Heat almost to boiling, but do not boil. Stir in the flaxseed oil just before serving.
Makes 8 servings. 140 calories, 8 g fat, 170 mg sodium.

Creamy Potato/Leek Soup

- ¼ cup vegetable stock
- 3¾ cup rinsed raw cashews
- 1½ cups leeks (white part only)
- 2 garlic cloves, crushed
- 4 cups vegetable stock
- 1½ pounds peeled, cubed potatoes
- ¼ cup sliced celery stalks
- 2 teaspoons Braggs Liquid Aminos
- ¼ teaspoon thyme
- 2 tablespoons nutritional yeast

- 1 can cannellini beans, drained
- 6 ounces fresh or canned kernel corn
- 2 tablespoons lignin-rich flaxseed oil

Blend stock and cashews until thick and smooth. Set aside. Combine the next seven ingredients and bring to a boil. Reduce and simmer gently approximately 15 minutes until vegetables are tender. Set aside one cup of the potatoes and leeks. Process remaining soup in batches until smooth, along with the yeast and cashew cream. Return the mixture to the soup pot and add the reserved potato and leek mixture and the beans and corn. Heat thoroughly, but do not boil. Stir in the flaxseed oil just before serving.
Makes 8 servings. 250 calories, 10 g fat, 520 mg sodium.

Spinach/Tofu Soup
• JUANITA ALEXANDER

- 2 tablespoons Braggs Liquid Aminos
- ½ pound firm tofu, cubed
- 3 cups water
- 3 cups Vegetable Stock (p. 38)
- ¾ cup brown rice
- 1 large Spanish onion, chopped
- 3 garlic cloves, minced
- 6 ounces fresh spinach, chopped
- ¼ cup thinly sliced green onions
- 1 tablespoon garlic powder
- 2 tablespoons nutritional yeast
- 2 tablespoons lignin-rich flaxseed oil

Marinate the tofu cubes in the aminos. Combine the next five ingredients in soup pot. Bring to a boil and simmer 20 minutes. Add the marinated tofu and cook an additional 15 minutes or until the rice is just cooked. Add the spinach and sliced green onions and garlic powder. Simmer three additional minutes. Stir in the yeast. Add the flaxseed oil just before serving.
Makes 4 servings. 310 calories, 12 g fat, 420 mg sodium.

Pumpkin Soup (Central America)
• JUANITA ALEXANDER

      2 cups water
      2 cups Vegetable Stock (p. 38)
      1 bag mixed vegetables
    1½ pounds pumpkin, chopped in large chunks
      1 large Spanish onion, chopped
      1 medium seeded green bell pepper, chopped
      6 peeled cloves of garlic
     ½ cup chopped cilantro
      1 pound diced coco malanga or all-purpose
        potatoes
      1 tablespoon Braggs Liquid Aminos
      1 can pinto beans
      1 can corn kernels
      3 tablespoons lignin-rich flaxseed

Cook the pumpkin chunks in the water and stock until the pumpkin is smooth. Blend together the onion, bell pepper, garlic, and cilantro. Add 3 tablespoons of the onion mixture to the pumpkin. Add the potatoes and the bag of mixed vegetables and simmer 20 minutes. Add the beans and the corn and simmer an additional 7 minutes. Adjust the seasonings. Stir in the flaxseed oil and serve.
Makes 6 servings. 340 calories, 8 g fat, 260 mg sodium.

Mock Chicken With Coconut Stew (Colombia)
• PAMELA WILLIAMS

        Vegetable oil spray
      1 medium onion, finely chopped
      2 cloves garlic, chopped
      1 green bell pepper, chopped
      2 12-ounce cans Worthington Low-Fat
        FriChik, drained and cut into chunks
      1 medium tomato, blanched, peeled, and
        chopped
      1 pimiento, chopped
     ¼ teaspoon salt
    1½ teaspoon McKay's Chicken Style Seasoning

    1½ cups water
      1 tablespoon water
      1 teaspoon cornstarch
     ½ cup coconut milk

Spray large saucepan with vegetable oil spray and sauté onions, garlic, and peppers. Add FriChik, tomatoes, pimiento, salt, McKay's Chicken Style Seasoning, and water. Bring to a boil, cover, and simmer for 30 minutes. Mix 1 tablespoon water with 1 teaspoon cornstarch and slowly add to saucepan while stirring. Continue stirring and add coconut milk. Stir for 5 minutes as sauce thickens. Serve with brown rice or couscous.
Makes 6 servings. 133 calories, 7 g fat, 571 mg sodium.

Herbal Stewed Eggplant
• JOCELYN M. PETERSON

      1 large eggplant, peeled and diced
      1 tablespoon turmeric
      1 onion, chopped
     ½ red bell pepper, diced
      2 tablespoons olive oil
      1 tablespoon cumin
      2 tablespoons parsley
      1 tablespoon sweet basil
      2 tablespoons chicken-style seasoning
      1 garlic clove, chopped
      1 cup water

Sauté onions, bell peppers, and garlic, then add chopped eggplant with turmeric and water. Simmer till eggplant is tender, then crush with a fork and add herbs and seasonings.
Makes 4 servings: 250 calories, 2 g fat, 150 mg sodium.

Callaloo Soup (Caribbean)
• JOHNETTA FRAZIER

- 1 bundle callaloo or one pound fresh spinach
- 6 okras, trimmed
- 1 plantain, cubed
- 1 teaspoon oregano
- 5 scallions, chopped
- 3 garlic cloves, minced
- 2 tablespoons chicken-style seasoning
- 1 pound yams, peeled and diced

Place all ingredients except yams in a pot with 2 quarts of boiling water. Allow to cook for 1½ hours over low to moderate heat. Let soup cool. Strain stock and set aside. Puree vegetables and return to pot with 2 cups of reserved stock. Slowly cook remaining stock in another pot and allow to reduce and thicken. While stock is reducing, cook yam in lightly salted water until tender. Add thickened stock and cooked yam to soup. Heat briefly and then serve immediately.
Makes 4 servings. 162 calories, 1 g fat, 162 mg sodium.

Sopa de Repollo (Cabbage Soup, Chile)
• PAMELA WILLIAMS

- 2 tablespoons butter
- 1 small green cabbage, finely shredded
- 1 large potato, grated
- 2 green onions, chopped
- 4 teaspoons McKay's Chicken Style Seasoning
- 4 cups water
  Cayenne pepper to taste
- ¼ cup plain bread crumbs
- ¼ cup mozzarella cheese, grated

In a large saucepan, add butter and place pan over medium heat. Add cabbage, potatoes, onions, and cook for five minutes or until cabbage is limp. Stir constantly. Mix chicken-style seasoning in ½ cup of water. Pour into saucepan. Add remaining water.

Simmer, covered, over a low heat for 30 minutes. Serve into soup bowls. Garnish with bread crumbs and mozzarella cheese.
Makes 6 servings. 108 calories, 5 g fat, 89 mg sodium.

Cauliflower Au Gratin Soup
• DONNA A. SMITH

- 1 tablespoon margarine
- 3 slices veggie cheese
- 1 cup nondairy sour cream
- 1 cup soy milk
- 1 10-ounce package chopped frozen cauliflower
- 1 teaspoon turmeric
- 1 teaspoon sweet basil
  Salt and cayenne pepper to taste

In a large skillet, melt margarine, cheese, and sour cream. Slowly add milk, then cauliflower and seasonings. Simmer until well seasoned and cauliflower is done.
Makes 6 servings. 112 calories, 8 g fat, 310 mg sodium.

Beef Barley Soup
• DONNA A. SMITH

- 1 cup dried barley
- 3 Prosage Patties, crumbled
- 1 32-ounce carton Imagine Natural Creamy Mushroom Soup
- 1 carrot, shredded
- 1-2 tablespoons margarine
  Salt and cayenne pepper to taste

Cook barley according to directions. Add sausage patties, mushroom soup, shredded carrots, margarine, and seasonings. Simmer until well seasoned.
Makes 6 servings. 242 calories, 6 g fat, 384 mg sodium.

Minestrone With Cabbage (Italy)

• ERMA WILLIAMS

    2 teaspoons olive oil
    2 cups shredded cabbage
    2 medium onions, chopped
    2 teaspoons minced garlic
 1½ cups water
 1½ teaspoons McKay's Beef Style Seasoning
    1 16-ounce can Italian-style stewed tomatoes
    1 cup red grape juice
    ½ cup sliced carrots
    ½ cup sliced celery
    1 16-ounce can kidney beans
    ½ cup diced zucchini
    2 teaspoons dried basil

    1 teaspoon dried oregano
    1 bay leaf
    ½ teaspoon salt
    1 cup cooked macaroni shells
    1 tablespoon chopped parsley
    2 teaspoons grated Parmesan cheese

In a 3-quart pot, heat oil. Add cabbage, onion, garlic, and cook over low to medium heat for 10 minutes. Stir to keep from sticking. Add broth, tomatoes, grape juice, carrots, and celery; cook for 20 minutes longer. Add beans, zucchini, and spices. Cook until tender, about 15 minutes longer. Add macaroni and cook 5 to 10 minutes longer. Sprinkle with parsley and Parmesan cheese.

Makes 10 servings. 140 calories, 4.2 g fat.

Minestrone Soup With Turnips (Italy)
• PAT HUMPHREY

- 3 tablespoons olive oil
- 2 medium onions, chopped
- 1 16-oz. can Italian-style stewed tomatoes
- 3 garlic cloves, minced
- 1 large carrot, sliced
- 2 small turnips, diced
- 2 stalks celery
- 5 cups vegetable stock (p. 38)
- 1 bay leaf
- 1 teaspoon dried oregano
- 1 teaspoon salt
- 1 16-ounce can kidney beans
- 1 8-ounce can garbanzo beans, undrained
- 1 cup elbow macaroni

Heat oil in a large soup pot. Add onion and sauté over medium-high heat for 2 to 3 minutes. Add tomatoes and garlic; cook 2 minutes. Add carrots, turnips, and celery and cook 3 more minutes, stirring occasionally. Add vegetable stock, bay leaf, oregano, and salt. Bring to a boil, then cover and cook over medium heat 15 minutes. Add kidney and garbanzo beans with liquid, cover, and simmer 10 minutes. Cook macaroni in another pot for 8 to 10 minutes. Drain and add to minestrone. Cook 5 minutes, then serve.
Makes 8 servings. 208 calories, 8 g fat, 624 mg sodium.

Peanut Stew Over Brown Rice (West Africa)
• PAMELA WILLIAMS

- 2 tablespoons oil
- 2 medium onions, cut into rings
- 2 medium green peppers, cut in strips
- 2 medium carrots, shredded
- ¾ cup peanut butter
- 6 ounces tomato paste
- 3 cups vegetable stock
- ½ teaspoon cayenne
- ½ teaspoon mace
- 4 medium potatoes, peeled, boiled, diced
- 3 cups cooked rice

Sauté onions, peppers, and carrots. Blend tomato paste with peanut butter; stir in vegetable stock (or 3 cups water plus 2 cubes Vegex dissolved in a small amount of hot water). Add seasonings. Add mixture to sautéed vegetables. Gently stir in potatoes. Stir over medium heat until heated through. Serve over brown rice.
Makes 8 serving. 476 calories, 18 g fat, 920 mg sodium.

Navy Bean Stew (Ethiopia)
• PAMELA WILLIAMS

- 1 cup dried navy beans
- 5 cups water
- 1 large onion, chopped
- 1 cup soy chunks, beef flavor
- 2 cloves garlic, chopped
- 2 large potatoes, peeled and cut into 1½ -inch squares
- 2 stalks celery, sliced into 1-inch chunks
- 2 carrots cut into 1-inch slices
- 1 cup corn cut off the cob
- ¼ teaspoon turmeric
- ¼ teaspoon coriander
- ¼ teaspoon cumin
- ¼ teaspoon ginger
- 1 teaspoon salt
- ½ pound fresh Brussel sprouts

Wash beans and boil for 30 minutes in a 3-quart saucepan. Remove from heat and let stand covered for 1 hour. Drain and add 5 cups water to beans. Set aside. Spray saucepan with vegetable oil and sauté onion until translucent. Add to beans. Add all ingredients except Brussels sprouts. Simmer for 1 hour or until beans are soft. Add sprouts and cook for 15 minutes longer. Serve hot.
Makes 6 servings. 231 calories, 2 g fat, 437 mg sodium.

Pigeon Pea Soup (Jamaica)
• PAT HUMPHREY

    1 onion, chopped
    1 tablespoon margarine
    1 cup pigeon peas, cooked
    1 cup canned corn
  2½ cups coconut milk

Cook onion in melted margarine until the onion is transparent. Add pigeon peas and corn and cook slowly for 10 minutes. Then place in blender, add coconut milk, season to taste, and blend thoroughly. Return mixture to cooking pan and heat gently for 20 minutes. Serve hot with bread.
Makes 4 servings. 593 calories, 39 g fat, 73 mg sodium.

Vegetable Stock
• JUANITA ALEXANDER

  15 cups of water
   2 leeks, chopped coarsely
   3 celery stalks, chopped coarsely
   2 tomatoes, unpeeled
   1 sweet bell pepper, chopped
   3 bay leaves
   1 sprig of fresh rosemary
   2 large onions with skin
   5 carrots, unpeeled
   3 garlic cloves
   1 parsnip, chopped
   3 sprigs of fresh thyme

In a large stockpot, bring the water to a boil. Add the vegetables and herbs and cook until tender and the liquid has reduced by one-third. Strain out the vegetables and herbs with cheesecloth or a fine sieve. Separate the stock into containers and freeze for later use.

While all nutritious foods contribute to healthy brain function, brain food for the vegetarian comes significantly in the form of flaxseed and lignin-rich flaxseed oil, known for its superior quality of omega-3 fatty acids; and from green leafy vegetables, legumes, nutritional (Brewer's) yeast, whole grains, and root vegetables known for their B-complex vitamins. Daily intake of these nutrient-dense foods achieves and maintains optimum function of neural circuits in the brain, as well as other bodily processes necessary for health.

Finger Food

Whether it's a lively Saturday night gathering or a formal dinner for two, be sure to include a selection of these enticing finger foods. Stuffed Cherry Tomatoes or Black Bean Dip make wonderful hors d'oeuvres for your guests. If it's a picnic you're planning, add creative flair to this culinary tradition with finger foods that are not only tasty but healthy.

Chick Nuggets
• PAT HUMPHREY

       16 ounces tofu, firm
        2 tablespoons McKay's Chicken Style Seasoning
       ½ cup wheat germ
        1 bottle barbecue sauce

Freeze tofu at least 24 hours. Thaw and squeeze out excess water. Cut into nugget-size pieces. Coat pieces with chicken-style seasoning, then toss with wheat germ. Bake at 350° F for 30 minutes. To serve, provide small bowls of barbecue sauce. Dip nuggets in sauce and eat.
Makes 4 servings. 263 calories, 13 g fat, 527 mg sodium.

Black Bean Dip
• PAMELA WILLIAMS

        1 16-ounce can black beans, drained
       ½ teaspoon ground cumin
       ½ teaspoon ground coriander
        1 garlic clove, finely chopped
        1 green onion, finely chopped
        2 teaspoons fresh lime or lemon juice
       ¼ teaspoon salt (or to taste)
           Cayenne pepper to taste (optional)

Place beans in bowl and mash with fork. Stir in remaining ingredients. Top with chopped green onions or light sour cream. Serve with tortilla chips.
Makes 4 servings. 101 calories, 0.5 g fat, 155 mg sodium.

Stuffed Cherry Tomatoes

       ½ pound cherry tomatoes
        8 ounces firm tofu, drained and crumbled
       ½ teaspoon oregano
       ½ teaspoon basil
       ¼ teaspoon garlic powder
       ¼ teaspoon onion powder
       ¼ teaspoon turmeric
           Dash of salt (or to taste)

Remove cherry tomato stems. Cut a small hole in the top of each tomato and remove and save the pulp. In a small bowl mix tomato pulp and the rest of the ingredients. Stuff tomatoes with the mixture. Chill and serve.
Makes 4 servings. 71 calories, 3.5 g fat, 13 mg sodium.

Sun, fun, beach—everyone loves picnics! Add creative flair to this summer tradition with foods that are not only tasty but healthy. Try Stuffed Pita Pockets or Petite Meatless Corned Beef Puffs on your next picnic.

Spinach Pate
• PAMELA WILLIAMS

- 2 10-ounce packages frozen chopped spinach
- ½ cup pine nuts
- 1 3-ounce package light cream cheese
- 1 small onion, diced
- 1 garlic clove, diced
- 1 teaspoon paprika
- 2 teaspoons dillweed
- 1 tablespoon lemon juice
- ½ teaspoon salt (or to taste)

In a medium saucepan, cook spinach as directed, drain, and cool. Squeeze out excess liquid with your hand and break spinach leaves into smaller pieces. Set aside. In a nonstick frying pan, toast pine nuts over low heat until golden brown. In a blender or food processor, combine pine nuts, light cream cheese, onion, garlic, paprika, dillweed, lemon juice, and salt. Puree to a paste. Mix with spinach until blended. Transfer to a serving bowl. Garnish with pine nuts and paprika. Refrigerate until serving time. Serve with crackers.
Makes 8 servings. 98 calories, 7.5 g fat, 70 mg sodium.

Tofu Kabobs
• PAMELA WILLIAMS

- 8 ounces extra-firm tofu
  Tamari sauce
- 4 tablespoons vegetable oil
- 2 tablespoons sesame seed oil
- ¼ teaspoon salt
- ½ teaspoon fresh ginger, grated
- 12 large mushrooms, washed and stems removed
- 1 green bell pepper, cut into 1 ½ -inch squares
- 12 pearl onions, peeled
- 1 cup pineapple chunks, drained

Cut tofu into 1½-inch squares. Lay squares on cookie sheet sprayed with vegetable cooking spray

and brush each square generously with tamari sauce. Place tofu under broiler until squares turn golden brown, about 3 to 5 minutes. Turn squares over and repeat. Remove squares from broiler. In a medium bowl, mix vegetable oil, sesame seed oil, salt, and ginger. Add mushrooms, bell pepper, and onions. Stir to coat vegetables. Marinate for 30 minutes to 2 hours. Thread equal amounts of vegetables, pineapple, and tofu on skewers. Set on baking sheet. Broil Kabobs about 4 inches from heat, 8 to 10 minutes, then serve.
Makes 6 servings. 191 calories, 16 g fat, 6 mg sodium.

Stuffed Grape Leaves
• PAMELA WILLIAMS

- 1 pound jar vine leaves
- 1½ tablespoons olive oil
- 1 medium onion, minced
- ½ cup pine nuts, toasted
- ¾ cup uncooked rice
- ½ cup currants
- 2½ cups water
- 2 tablespoons fresh parsley, finely chopped
- ¼ teaspoon salt

½ teaspoon cinnamon
¼ teaspoon allspice
2 tomatoes, peeled, seeded, chopped
2 tablespoons lemon juice
3 tablespoons olive oil

Unfold vine leaves and rinse under cold water; drain. Heat olive oil in saucepan. Add onion and sauté on low heat until onion is translucent. Add pine nuts, rice, currants, and 1¼ cups water. Cover and cook for 20 minutes or until liquid is absorbed. Stir in parsley, salt, cinnamon, allspice, and tomatoes. With stem end of leaf toward you, place approximately 1 round tablespoon of filling on each vine leaf. Fold sides to center and roll. Lay rolls with seam down so they will not come apart. Place thin layer of unfilled vine leaves in bottom of large saucepan. Tightly pack filled rolls in pan, seam down, in layers. Sprinkle with lemon juice and 3 tablespoons oil. Add 1 cup water; place a plate on top of rolls to weigh them down. Cover and bring to a boil. Reduce heat and cook 30 minutes, Remove from heat and cool. Serve cold.
Makes 10 servings (4 per serving). 177 calories, 10g fat, 180 mg sodium.

Stuffed Zucchini
• PAMELA WILLIAMS

3 medium zucchini, unpeeled
4 ounces soft low-fat cream cheese
3 Stripples, crumbles
2 cloves garlic, minced
2 tablespoons onion, minced
1 tablespoon parley, finely chopped
Cayenne pepper

Cut off zucchini ends; scoop out the center with spoon. Mix remaining ingredients. Pack mixture into center of zucchini with spoon. Chill. Cut into half-inch slices.
Makes 6 servings. 80 calories, 5.5 g fat, 141 mg sodium.

Eggplant Pizza
• PAMELA WILLIAMS

1 medium eggplant
Olive oil spray
1 large tomato, thinly sliced
½ teaspoon oregano
½ teaspoon basil
¼ teaspoon cumin
½ cup soy cheese, grated

Peel and cut eggplant into ¼-inch-thick round slices. Sprinkle both sides of eggplant with a little salt. Let stand for 10 minutes, rinse, and pat dry. Spray cookie sheet with olive oil spray and place eggplant on cookie sheet. Broil about 4 inches from heat until light brown. Turn and brown other side until light brown. Remove eggplant from oven. Reduce oven temperature to 350° F. Top each eggplant slice with a tomato slice. Sprinkle with herbs, and top with a little cheese. Return to oven and bake 5 minutes. Serve immediately.
Makes 6 servings. 99 calories, 6 g fat, 121 mg sodium.

Vegetable Fondue
• PAMELA WILLIAMS

1 pound broccoli, cut into florets
8 ounces mushrooms
1 bunch green onions, cut into ½-inch pieces
6 teaspoons McKay's Chicken Style Seasoning
8 cups water
4 tablespoons soy sauce
4 cloves garlic, minced
Cayenne pepper

Arrange first three ingredients on serving tray. Mix chicken seasoning and 1 cup of water. Pour this mixture and remaining ingredients into an electric skillet and heat mixture to 225° F. Guests spear vegetables with fondue forks and cook in broth for 1 to 2 minutes. Serve with garlic toast.
Makes 8 servings. 32 calories, 0 g fat, 310 mg sodium.

Greek Spinach Turnovers (Greece)

• PAMELA WILLIAMS

- 1 egg (or egg substitute equivalent)
  Medium onion, finely chopped
- ¼ pound low-fat cottage cheese
- 4 ounces cream cheese
- 5 ounces frozen chopped spinach, thawed and drained (squeeze out excess water)
- 2 tablespoons parsley, chopped
- ¼ teaspoon dillweed
- 2 cloves garlic, minced
- 6 sheets phyllo dough
  Olive oil spray

In mixing bowl, add the following ingredients one at a time—egg, onion, cottage cheese, cream cheese, spinach, and seasonings. Blend well. Chill for 1 hour. Phyllo dough must be handled with great care and must be covered with a moist towel to keep from drying. Carefully remove six sheets and cut into strips 2 inches wide and 16 inches long. Spray olive oil on each sheet. Place 1 teaspoon of filling on one end of strip. Fold one corner of strip to opposite side, forming a triangle and enclosing filling. Continue to fold in the same manner to the end of the strip, maintaining the shape of a triangle. Spray with olive oil. Place on an ungreased cookie sheet and bake for 20 minutes in oven preheated to 375° F. Serve.
Makes 30 servings. 30 calories, 2 g fat, 50 mg sodium.

Petite Meatless Corned Beef Puffs

• PAMELA WILLIAMS

- 1 cup water
- ½ cup olive oil
- 1 cup enriched flour, sifted
- ⅛ teaspoon salt
- 4 eggs (or egg substitute equivalent)
- ½ cup Worthington Meatless Corned Beef®, finely chopped
- ⅛ teaspoon basil
  Parmesan cheese
  Basil

Bring water and olive oil to a boil. Add flour and salt all at once. Reduce heat and cook while continuously stirring. Cook until smooth and mixture forms a small ball (about 1 to 2 minutes). Remove from heat and cool until warm. Add eggs one at a time, beating well after each addition. Place batter into a mixing bowl and mix in corned beef. Drop by teaspoonsful into half-inch piles on greased baking sheet. Bake in preheated oven for 20 minutes a 350° F or until golden brown and firm to touch. Remove and sprinkle with Parmesan cheese and basil. Serve warm or cold.
Makes 9 dozen. 206 calories, 15 g fat, 117 mg sodium.

Tofu Spread

• PAMELA WILLIAMS

- 8 ounces firm tofu, mashed
- 1 large avocado, mashed
- 4 teaspoons tamari or low-sodium soy sauce
- 2 teaspoons lemon juice
- ¼ teaspoon paprika
- ¼ teaspoon onion powder

Mix tofu and avocado in a bowl. Add the rest of the ingredients. Spread on whole-grain bread or crackers. Garnish with olives or pimientos.
Makes 6 servings: 72 calories, 5.5 g fat, 133 mg sodium.

Olive Spread

• PAT HUMPHREY

- 1 cup black olives, chopped
- ½ cup walnuts, finely chopped
- ¼ cup almonds, finely chopped
- ¼ cup sesame or sunflower seeds
- ¼ cup celery, finely chopped
  Tofu Mayonnaise (p. 51, 52, 65)

Mix first five ingredients in bowl, adding enough mayonnaise to allow mixture to spread easily.
Makes 8 servings. 117 calories, 11.4 g fat, 482 mg sodium.

Garbanzo Spread

• PAT HUMPHREY

- 1 15-ounce can garbanzos, mashed well with fork
- 1 tablespoon soy mayonnaise
- 1 tablespoon chopped onions
- 1 tablespoon chopped green peppers
- 1 chopped garlic clove
- 1 teaspoon parsley flakes
- ¼ teaspoon basil
- 1 teaspoon Vegit Seasoning
- ¼ teaspoon turmeric

Mix all ingredients together and serve with bread or crackers.
Makes 8 servings. 80 calories, 3 g fat, 100 mg sodium.

Avocado Spread

• PAT HUMPHREY

- 1 ripe avocado
- 1 teaspoon garlic powder
- Dash of lemon juice
- Salt to taste

Mash avocado, then add garlic powder, lemon juice, and salt. Serve as garnish for haystacks, or spread on crackers, bread, or rice cakes.
Makes 6 servings. 104 calories, 10.9 g fat, 84 mg sodium.

Hummus

• PAT HUMPHREY

- 1 15-ounce can chickpeas, drained (save liquid)
- ¼ cup tahini (sesame seed butter)
- 2 medium cloves garlic, minced
- 3 tablespoons lemon juice
- 1 teaspoon onion powder
- 1 teaspoon salt
- Dried, chopped parsley

Blend all ingredients in food processor, adding liquid only as needed to make a smooth paste. Add chopped parsley as desired. Keep chilled.
Makes 16 servings. 107 calories, 3.6 g fat, 136 mg sodium.

Fresh Soy Nuts

• PAMELA WILLIAMS

- 1 cup dried soybeans
- 6 cups water

Soak dry soybeans in 3 cups of water overnight. Drain. In a large pot, heat 3 cups of water and 1 cup of soybeans to boiling and cook for 60 minutes. Drain beans and cool. Heat oven to 350° F. Spread beans in a single layer on a large baking sheet. Bake for 30 minutes, stirring every 10 minutes or so. Cool and season to taste. Store in tightly covered jar.
Makes 2 to 3 cups or 6 servings. 141 calories, 6 g fat, 2 mg sodium.

Egg Salad Sandwich Filling

• PAT HUMPHREY

- 1 pound tofu, mashed
- McKay's Chicken Style Seasoning
- ⅓ cup olives, chopped
- 1 tablespoon Tofu Mayonnaise (p. 51, 52, 65)

Sauté tofu in a nonstick skillet coated with vegetable spray. Add chicken-style seasoning to taste. Add chopped olives and moisten with Tofu Mayonnaise.
Makes 6 servings. 79 calories, 5.7 g fat, 295 mg sodium.

Veggie Big Boy

• PAT HUMPHREY

- 6 tablespoons mayonnaise
- 4 teaspoons PA's Pickle Smack relish
- 4 teaspoons tomato sauce
- 4 whole wheat buns
- 4 Oat Pecan Burgers (p. 90)
- 2 tomatoes, sliced
- 4 slices Jack Cheeze (p. 51)
- 1 cup lettuce, shredded
  Salt

Mix mayonnaise (preferably low-fat, dairy-free), relish, and tomato sauce. Toast buns, then spread sauce on top and bottom buns. Place burger on bottom bun, then top with tomato, slice of Jack Cheeze, and shredded lettuce.
Makes 4 servings.

English Muffin Pizzas

• PAT HUMPHREY

- ¼ cup onion, chopped
- ¼ cup bell pepper, chopped
- ¼ teaspoon basil
- ¼ teaspoon oregano
- ¼ teaspoon garlic powder
- ½ cup black olives, sliced
- 1 cup pizza sauce (canned or homemade)
- 1 package whole-grain English Muffins
- 1 cup grated Jack Cheese

Sauté onion and green pepper in small amount of water with basil, oregano, and garlic powder for about 1 minute. Add olives and tomato sauce to mixture. Cover English muffin halves with sauce and top with grated Jack Cheese. Bake until hot and bubbly.
Makes 12 servings. 99 calories (without cheese), 2.6 g fat, 370 mg sodium.

Corn-Salsa Pita Sandwiches

• PAT HUMPHREY

Sandwiches

- 4 ears of corn
- 1½ cups red cabbage, shredded
- 1 green bell pepper, chopped
- 1 tomato, chopped
- 6 Worthington® Breakfast Strips, cooked
- 6 whole wheat pitas
- 1½ cups veggie slices tofu cheese (cheddar style), shredded

Salsa

- 1 cup Sour Supreme (sour cream substitute)
- 3 tablespoons lime juice
- 2 tablespoons chopped onions
- 1 garlic clove, minced
- 1 teaspoon chili powder
- 1 teaspoon ground cumin
- ½ teaspoon honey
- ¼ teaspoon salt
- ¼ teaspoon cayenne pepper

Mix all salsa ingredients well and chill. Remove husks and silk from corn and snap off ends of stalks. Drop corn ears in salted water, boiling rapidly. Cover, and cook for 5 to 7 minutes. Remove corn from water, drain, and cut corn from cob. Combine finely shredded cabbage, green pepper, tomato, and cooked crumbled Breakfast Strips into a large bowl. Stir in ¾ cup of salsa mix, blending well. Cover and chill mixture. When ready to serve, fill pita bread with corn mixture; top with remaining salsa and shredded tofu cheese.
Makes 6 servings. 444 calories, 11g fat, 721 mg sodium.

Soy Burgers
• PAMELA WILLIAMS

- 1 green pepper, finely chopped
- 1 celery stalk, finely chopped
- 2 green onions, finely chopped
- 1 tablespoon parsley, chopped
- 1 cup cooked soybeans, mashed with a fork
- 1 cup cooked brown rice
- 2 eggs (or egg substitute equivalent), lightly beaten
- ¾ cup plain low-fat or nonfat yogurt
- ¼ teaspoon thyme
  Dash of cayenne pepper

In a small saucepan, sauté green pepper and celery for 1 minute. Cool. In a mixing bowl combine all ingredients and let stand for 15 minutes. Form small patties. Fry patties in a non-stick saucepan sprayed with vegetable cooking spray. Serve covered with gravy or in sandwiches with garnish.
Makes 4 servings. 198 calories, 6 g fat, 210 mg sodium.

Tofu Burgers With Cheese
• PAMELA AND ERMA WILLIAMS

- 1 pound firm tofu
- 2 cups mashed potatoes
- ¼ cup mozzarella cheese or soy cheese
- 1 cup chopped green onion
- ½ cup seasoned Italian bread crumbs
  Nonstick cooking spray

Drain tofu and pat dry. Cut tofu into small squares. Combine tofu, potatoes, cheese, and green onions. Shape into six patties. Cover patties in bread crumbs. Spray skillet with nonstick spray and cook patties over low heat for 5 minutes or until brown. Spray pan again and brown other side of patty, then serve.
Makes 6 servings. 127 calories, 5.5g fat.

Tofu Burgers With Cornmeal
• PAT HUMPHREY

- 2 pounds tofu, mashed
- 2 cups whole wheat bread crumbs
- 1 tablespoon soy sauce
- 1 teaspoon garlic powder
- 1 teaspoon salt
- ½ cup celery, finely chopped
- 2 teaspoons onion powder
- ½ cup cornmeal
- ½ cup oat flour (made in blender)
- ¼ teaspoon salt

Mix well first seven ingredients and form into patties. Mix cornmeal, flour, and salt. Roll patties. Roll patties in this mixture. Brown in nonstick pan coated with Pam. Serve on sesame bun with lettuce, tomato, and soy mayonnaise.
Makes 16 burgers. 194 calories, 2 g fat, 503 mg sodium.

Tofu Burgers With Egg Beaters
• CHRISTINA FLEMING-GABRIEL

- 1 pound soft tofu, drained
- 1 medium onion, chopped
- ½ teaspoon each; garlic powder, basil, oregano, and crushed red pepper
- ¼ cup Egg Beaters
- ⅓ cup plain bread crumbs
- 1 tablespoon vegetable oil

Mash tofu in a medium-size bowl. Add chopped onions, seasonings, egg substitute, and bread crumbs. Combine all ingredients thoroughly. Meanwhile, heat a skillet with one tablespoon of vegetable oil. Form tofu mixture into medium size patties and place in heated skillet. Brown on both sides and drain on paper towel. Place tofu burger on bun with sautéed red onion, sliced tomatoes, and lettuce.
Makes 4 servings. 114 calories, 2.2 g fat, 44 mg sodium.

Tofu Burgers With Celery

2 pounds tofu, mashed
2 cups whole wheat
1 tablespoon soy sauce
1 teaspoon garlic powder
1 teaspoon salt
½ cup celery, finely chopped
2 teaspoons onion powder
½ cup cornmeal
½ up oat flour (made in blender)
¼ teaspoon salt

Mix well first seven ingredients and form into patties. Mix cornmeal, flour, and salt. Roll patties in this mixture. Brown in nonstick pan coated with nonstick spray. Serve on sesame bun with lettuce, tomato, and soy mayonnaise
Makes 16 servings. 194 calories, 2 g fat, 503 mg sodium.

Tofu Burgers With Vege-Sal

• JOCELYN PETERSON

1 pound soft tofu
1 tablespoon grated onion
¼ cup wheat germ
½ teaspoon garlic powder
¼ cup whole wheat flour
½ teaspoon Vege-Sal
2 tablespoons nutritional yeast
¼ teaspoon cumin

Mix and mash all ingredients together in a bowl. Form into six 3-inch burgers. Brown on each side in 1 tablespoon olive oil. Serve hot on a bun, either plain or "with all the fixings."
Makes 6 servings. 119 calories, 6 g fat, 8 g protein, 9 g carbohydrate, 85 mg sodium.

Black Bean Burgers

• PAT HUMPHREY

2 15-ounce cans black beans
2 medium onions, chopped
½ cup parsley, chopped
½ cup pistachio nuts, ground
1 tablespoon olive oil
1 teaspoon salt
2 tablespoons wheat germ
¼ teaspoon cayenne pepper
1 tablespoon Braggs Liquid Aminos
1 teaspoon cumin, ground
1 cup herb-seasoned stuffing cubes

In food processor or blender process beans with liquid. Place in bowl. Add chopped onions, parsley, and ground pistachios and mix well. Add remaining ingredients and form into hamburger-size patties. Brown about 5 to 6 minutes on each side in skillet coated with vegetable spray. Serve on whole wheat buns topped with sliced tomatoes, avocado, sprouts, and salsa.
Makes 8 servings. 459 calories, 6 g fat, 480 mg sodium.

Oven-Baked Fries

• PAT HUMPHREY

¼ cup olive oil
1 tablespoon Tone's garlic and herb seasoning
1 tablespoon McKay's Chicken Style Seasoning
2 pounds potatoes, cut into wedges

Preheat oven to 450° F. Mix oil and seasonings in large bowl. Add potatoes and toss to coat. Place potatoes on baking sheet and roast for 20 to 25 minutes. Watch carefully; turn pieces so all surfaces brown.
Makes 6 servings. 174 calories, 9 g fat, 165 mg sodium.

Nachos and Cheeze
• PAT HUMPHREY

- 1 medium bell pepper
- ½ cup food yeast flakes
- ⅓ cup tomato juice
- 3 cups water
- ¼ cup soy milk powder
- 2 tablespoons cornstarch
- 2¼ teaspoon salt
- ¼ teaspoon garlic powder
- ¼ teaspoon onion powder
- ⅓ cup flour
- 1 bag baked or regular tortilla chips
- ¼ cup tahini

Chop pepper and sauté in small amount of water. Blend at high speed all ingredients except tortilla chips, tahini and about 4 tablespoons of the chopped pepper. Cook this mixture until well thickened, stirring constantly. Mix in tahini. Put chips on cookie sheet and pour sauce over them. Top with chopped pepper. Place chips under broiler until cheese melts. Watch carefully. Serve immediately.
Makes 10 servings. 74 calories, 3 g fat, 528 mg sodium.

Stuffed Pita Pockets (Near East)
• PAT HUMPHREY

- 1 bunch fresh spinach, washed, stemmed, and coarsely chopped
- ¼ cup chopped black olives
- ½ cucumber, peeled and chopped
- ½ green bell pepper, cored, seeded, and chopped
- 1 bunch green onions, chopped
- ½ cup cooked garbanzo beans
- 2 cups chopped tomatoes
- 1 cup chopped avocado
  Tofu Mayonnaise (p. 51, 52, 65)
  Salt, to taste
  Whole wheat pita pockets
  Alfalfa sprouts

Mix all ingredients together lightly except for pita bread and sprouts, using enough mayonnaise to moisten. Stuff mixture into pita pockets and garnish with alfalfa sprouts.
Makes 6 servings. 421 calories, 16 g fat, 691 mg sodium.

Dips and

Smooth, creamy, tangy—these are just some of the adjectives that may pop into your mind when you think of a delicious spread for a sandwich or a dip for fresh veggies. How about a dairy-free "cheeze" that slices and melts like a dream? You'll be glad to know there is a way to have ketchup without all the commercial additives. This section contains some mouth-watering recipes for the healthiest, most tasty dips and spreads.

Spreads

Jack Cheeze
• PAT HUMPHREY

¾ cup cooked millet
2 tablespoons plain kosher gelatin
1 cup cold water
¼ cup raw cashews, rinsed
¼ cup nutritional yeast flakes
¼ cup lemon juice
1 teaspoon salt
1 teaspoon onion powder
¼ teaspoon garlic powder

To cook millet, add 1 cup dry millet and 1 teaspoon salt to 4 cups boiling water. Reduce heat and cook for 45 to 60 minutes or until water is absorbed. (Can substitute brown rice for millet.) Mix gelatin in water and allow to soften 5 minutes. Heat mixture in saucepan until dissolved and clear. Blend gelatin mixture along with remaining ingredients. Place in a small bread pan or mold and chill several hours. Then slice, grate, or cut into cubes. Melts when exposed to heat. (If you plan to make cheeze ahead and freeze, replace millet with 1 cup cashews.)
Makes 16 servings. 42 calories, 1.9 g fat, 128 mg sodium.

Tofu Mayonnaise 1
• DONNA GREEN GOODMAN

1 pound crumbled tofu
½ cup water
1 teaspoon salt
2½ teaspoons onion powder
¼ cup honey (optional)
1 teaspoon garlic powder
½ cup canola oil
½ cup lemon juice
   Nutritional yeast flakes
   Bakon seasoning
   Turmeric

Rinse, drain, crumble, and measure tofu. Put into blender and add remaining ingredients. Add flakes, Bakon seasoning, and turmeric to taste. Blend on high for 1 minute until creamy. Keep refrigerated.
Makes 2 ½ cups. 38 calories, 4 g fat, 60 mg sodium.

Some Tips for Dips:

• Estimate serving sizes. The number of servings depends on your guests' appetites but in general, estimate 1/4 cup dip per person.

• Mix before you serve. Most serving bowls are the wrong size and shape for mixing. Stir the dip in a mixing bowl and then transfer it to a serving bowl.

• Let it rest. Some dips benefit from a resting period before serving. Others, such as guacamole and some salsas, are best served right away; if they sit too long, the flavors get muddled.

• Don't forget the garnish. Make it look as good as it tastes with a sprinkle of paprika, a drizzle of olive oil, fresh herbs, or a dollop of soy yogurt.

• Think outside the bowl. Choose a brightly-colored bowl to set off the dip. Or get creative with hollowed-out loaves of bread, heads of cabbage, or winter squash.

www.bhg.com/recipes/10-tips-for-dips/

Soy Mayonnaise 1
• PAMELA WILLIAMS

          1 cup water
         ¾ teaspoon salt
         ½ teaspoon garlic powder
         ½ teaspoon onion powder
         ½ cup fresh lemon juice
         ½ cup soy flour
         ½ cup soy protein powder
        1½ cups soy oil
         ½ cup canola oil

Blend salt, garlic, onion, lemon juice, flour, protein powder, water, and ½ cup of the oil until well mixed, using lowest speed on blender. Slowly add the remaining oil while blender is still on low speed. Blend until the mixture is smooth and thick. Chill. Makes about 2 cups.
Makes 32 servings. 129 calories, 13.5 fat, 29 mg sodium.

Tofu Mayonnaise 2
• PAT HUMPHREY

          1 10.5-ounce package tofu
         ⅛ cup water
         ½ teaspoon salt
         ⅛ teaspoon garlic powder
          1 teaspoon onion powder
         ⅛ teaspoon basil
          3 tablespoons honey
         ⅓ cup lemon juice
         ⅓ cup raw cashews, rinsed

Blend all ingredients except tofu. When smooth, add tofu and blend. Chill.
Makes 6 servings. 42 calories, 2.5 g fat, 51 mg sodium.
NOTE: See Salads (p. 58) for additional tofu and soy mayonnaise recipes.

Corn Butter
• PAT HUMPHREY

         ½ cup hot cooked grits
          1 cup fresh or frozen corn
         ½ cup water
        1¼ teaspoon salt
          1 tablespoon oil

Cook grits according to package directions. In another pot, cook corn 8 minutes in water. Blend corn, grits, salt, and oil until smooth. Add water if needed to achieve a butter like consistency.
Makes 16 servings. 23 calories, 0.4 g fat, 31 mg sodium.

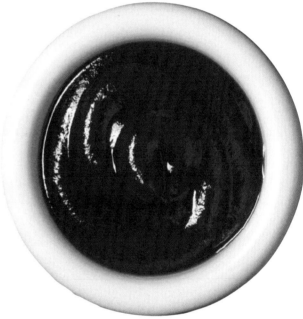

Fresh Ketchup
• PAMELA AND ERMA WILLIAMS

          1 onion, chopped
          2 cloves of garlic, chopped
          5 tablespoons apple juice concentrate
          1 small can tomato paste
         ½ cup lemon juice
         ¼ teaspoon ground cinnamon
         ⅛ teaspoon ground cloves
         ½ teaspoon paprika

Place all ingredients in a food processor or blender. Blend until smooth.
Makes 1½ cups ketchup. 260 calories, 0 g fat.

Basil Pesto
• BARBARA FRAZIER

¼ cup pine nuts
3 cups dry basil leaves
2 tablespoons garlic powder
4 tablespoons extra-virgin olive oil
2 teaspoons Braggs's liquid Aminos

Grind pine nuts in hand food mill, food grinder, or mortar and pestle. Add other ingredients. Mix vigorously with wire whip.
Makes 4 servings. 186 calories, 20 g fat, 3 g protein, 70 mg sodium.

Banana Chutney
• PAMELA WILLIAMS

1 pound white onions, minced
3 cloves garlic, minced
¾ pound pitted dates, chopped
6 ripe bananas, mashed
1½ cups lemon juice
1 teaspoon freshly grated ginger
1 cup pineapple juice
¼ cup lime juice
½ teaspoon salt
3 whole cloves
Cayenne pepper to taste (optional)

In a large, heavy pot, combine onions, garlic, and dates, and cook over medium heat for 3 minutes, stirring constantly. Stir in bananas and lemon juice, bring to a boil, cover and simmer for 20 minutes. Add raisins, ginger, pineapple juice, lime juice, salt, cloves, and cayenne pepper. Bring to a boil over a moderate heat and cook for 10 minutes.
Cool and store in sterilized jars.
Makes 2 quarts (24 servings).
Per serving: 70 calories, 0 g fat, 50 mg sodium.

Barbeque Sauce
• DONNA A. SMITH

1 medium onion, minced
2 garlic cloves, minced
⅓ cup oil
2 8-ounce cans low-sodium tomato sauce
¼ cup water
1 cup brown sugar
1 tablespoon molasses
1 teaspoon salt
¾ teaspoon cayenne pepper
½ cup lemon juice
1 tablespoon soy sauce

Sauté onion and garlic in oil. Add remaining ingredients except for lemon juice and soy sauce. Bring mixture to boil, reduce heat, and simmer for 30 minutes. Add lemon juice and soy sauce.
Makes 2 cups (nutrient analysis based on ¼ cup).
207 calories, 9 g fat, 394 mg sodium.

Beverages

There's nothing more refreshing than a cool drink on a hot afternoon. We've collected a few of our favorites with delightful mixtures of chunks of fresh fruit, ice, honey and natural fruit juices. These beverages will complete a power breakfast, compliment a casual summer meal or stand alone as a filling treat. Kids will love 'em and you can be sure these drinks are healthy, quick, and easy. Drink up!

Tropical Smoothie
• PAT HUMPHREY

  2½ cups unsweetened pineapple juice, chilled
    1 cup strawberries, sliced
    1 banana, sliced or
    1 mango, diced or
    1 papaya, diced

Peel and dice the fruit. Combine all ingredients in blender. Puree until thick and very smooth. Serve in glass. Garnish with whole strawberry and perhaps mint sprig. Hint: If using mangoes or papayas, be sure they are ripe.
Makes 4 servings. 115 calories, less than 1 g fat, 2 mg sodium.

Tropical Sorbet (South America)
• PAMELA WILLIAMS

    2 cups water
   ¾ cup raw sugar
    1 large ripe mango
    1 large ripe papaya

In a saucepan, combine water and sugar. Bring to a boil over medium heat and stir until sugar is dissolved. Remove from heat and cool. Peel mango and papaya, cut meat into chunks, and puree in blender (make sure seeds are removed from papaya). Slowly add sugar water and continue to puree until blended. Cover and chill. Remove and process the chilled puree in an ice-cream maker according to manufacturer's directions. Serve.
Makes 4 servings. 208 calories, 0 g fat, 4 mg sodium.

Banana Strawberry Shake
• PAMELA WILLIAMS

    4 very ripe bananas
  12 ripe or frozen whole strawberries
    1 tablespoon unsweetened strawberry preserves
   ¼ cup trail mix

Peel bananas and cut into thirds. Wrap bananas and strawberries in wax paper and freeze. Remove bananas and strawberries from freezer and let thaw for 10 minutes. Place in a food processor and blend for 4 minutes, until creamy. Place mixture in serving dishes and top with preserves. Sprinkle with trail mix.
Makes 8 serving. 85 calories, 2 g fat, 2 mg sodium.

The high intake of sugar-sweetened drinks has been a driving force behind the high incidence of obesity among our children. Did you know that one 12-ounce can of soda has 10 teaspoons of sugar? Soda drinkers are also more likely to have a lower intake of important nutrients, such as vitamin C, vitamin A, folate, magnesium, and calcium. The decrease in calcium can result in reduced bone mass, which can contribute to broken bones in children and can possibly lead to osteoporosis later in life.

womenshealth.about.com
"You Are Why You Drink"

Beverages

Yogurt Fruit Shakes

    1 cup fresh fruit (peaches, strawberries,
      bananas, papaya, or mango, etc.)
    1 cup nonfat yogurt, freeze
    ¼ cup of peach nectar
      Cran-strawberry juice
      Papaya or mango nectar
    1 teaspoon honey

Combine and blend ingredients in blender until smooth. Serve and top with sprig of mint, fresh berries, or a twist of lemon or orange slice.
Makes 2 servings. 146 calories (varies), 0 g fat.

Strawberry Soy Milk Shake

• JOCELYN M. PETERSON
    1 cup soy milk
    1 cup fresh strawberries
    1 teaspoon honey
    ½ cup crushed ice

Blend together until smooth.
Makes 1 serving. 150 calories, 3 g fat, 10 mg sodium.

Spanish Fresh Fruit Frappe

• PAT HUMPHREY
    1 cup watermelon, diced
    1 cup cantaloupe, cubed
    1 cup pineapple, diced
    1 cup mangoes, sliced
    1 cup strawberries, halved
    1 cup orange juice
    ¼ cup honey
      Crushed ice

Mix all ingredients. Fill blender half full of mixture and fill to top with crushed ice. Cover and blend on high speed until uniform consistency is achieved. Repeat with remaining mixture. Serve immediately, garnishing with fresh fruit if desired.
Makes 6 servings. 86 calories, less than 1 g fat, 3 mg sodium.

Watermelon Slush

• PAMELA WILLIAMS
    1 cup watermelon, squared and seeded
    ½ cup crushed ice
    1 teaspoon fresh lemon juice
    1 teaspoon raw sugar

Place ingredients in blender and blend until smooth.
Makes 2 servings. 55 calories, 5 g fat, 4 mg sodium.

Double "Chocolate" Shake

• PAT HUMPHREY
    1 cup water
    3 bananas, frozen
    2 tablespoons Better Than Milk powder
    2 tablespoons carob powder
    1 teaspoon honey or sucanot (optional)

Place all ingredients in blender and whiz at high speed. Serve immediately.
Makes 2 servings. 203 calories, 6 g fat, 5 mg sodium.

Mango Smoothie

• JOHNETTA FRAZIER
    2 ripe mangos, sliced
    1 12-ounce can pineapple-orange juice
      concentrate
    2 cups crushed ice

Place ingredients in blender and blend.
Makes 6 servings. 165 calories, 0 g fat, 15 mg sodium.

Almond Nut Milk

• JOCELYN M. PETERSON
    1 cup almonds
    4 cups cold water

Blend above ingredients thoroughly until smooth.
Makes 5 cups. 120 calories, trace sodium.

Fruit Smoothie
• RUTH DAVIS

2 bananas, peeled
1 cup strawberries, hulled
4 cups orange juice
8 ice cubes (optional)

Place all ingredients in a blender and blend until smooth. Serve chilled as desired; ice cubes will give a frothy texture. Other fruits may be substituted as desired.
Makes 4 servings. 174 calories, 0.77 g fat, 2.75 mg sodium

Fruit Smoothie
• DONNA GREEN GOODMAN

2 bananas
1 cup unsweetened crushed pineapple in its own juice
1 cup unsweetened sliced strawberries
1 cup soy milk
1 teaspoon alcohol-free vanilla flavoring
½ teaspoon alcohol-free coconut flavoring
1 tablespoon honey
Ice (optional)

Blend ingredients until smooth and serve cold.
Makes 8 servings. 70 calories, less than 1 g fat, 13 mg sodium.

Iced Herb Tea
• DONNA GREEN GOODMAN

1 gallon water
8 caffeine-free herbal tea bags (Wild Berry Zinger, Caribbean Kiwi-peach, and CranRazz Sunsets are excellent choices.)
1 12-ounce can 100 percent white grape juice concentrate

To one gallon of water add 8 tea bags. Let steep in the refrigerator at least 4 hours. Sweeten to taste with one can juice concentrate.
Makes 8 servings. 20 calories, 0 g fat, 3 mg sodium.

Citrus Fizz
• PAMELA AND ERMA WILLIAMS

2 cups pineapple juice
2 cups orange juice
1 6-ounce can frozen lemonade concentrate
1 28-ounce bottled sparkling water

Combine ingredients in a pitcher and serve immediately.
Makes 8 servings. 103 calories, 0 g fat.

Tropical Mint-Ade
• PAMELA AND ERMA WILLIAMS

2 bunches of fresh mint
3 cups water
¼ cup honey
¼ cup lemon juice
1 cup grapefruit juice
1 cup orange juice
2 tablespoons chopped pineapple

Wash mint and place in saucepan. Add 1 cup water and honey. Bring to a boil and simmer uncovered 10 minutes. Chill, then strain mint syrup. Add lemon, grapefruit, and orange juices, pineapple, and remaining water to mint syrup. Pour over ice in tea glasses. Garnish with mint sprigs.
Makes 8 servings. 52 calories, 0 g fat.

Salads and

ooking for the perfect compliment to that special meal you've planned? Or maybe you want to shrink your waistline by cutting back on calories. Try a salad! The salads on the following pages are perfect as an accompaniment to any meal—or as a light meal in themselves!

VEGETABLE SALADS

Zesty Green Salad
• ERMA WILLIAMS

- ½ head of green leaf lettuce
- ½ head of butter head lettuce
- ½ bunch fresh parsley
- 4 tablespoons fresh dill leaves, chopped
- 1 red tomato, cut into wedges
- ½ cucumber, peeled and sliced
- 2 tablespoons olive oil
- 1 teaspoon fresh lemon juice
- Salt to taste

Wash and break lettuce leaves into bite-size pieces. Remove parsley leaves from stems. Combine lettuce, parsley, dill, tomato, and cucumber in a large salad bowl. Combine olive oil and lemon juice and spoon over salad. Season with salt. Toss and serve.
Makes 4 servings. 79 calories, 7 g fat.

Italian Tossed Salad (Italy)
• PAT HUMPHREY

- 1 bunch each of Romaine, Boston, red leaf lettuce
- 1 bunch green onions, chopped
- 1 cucumber, sliced
- 2 carrots, grated
- 1 stalk celery, diced
- 4 radishes, sliced
- ½ green pepper, diced
- ½ cup parsley, chopped

DRESSING

- 1 tablespoon lemon juice
- ½ teaspoon garlic powder
- ½ teaspoon oregano
- Dash of salt

Toss first eight items together, then garnish with lemon juice, garlic powder, oregano, and salt.
Makes 10 servings. 25 calories, 0 g fat, 17 mg sodium.

Not only do salads taste good (especially on hot days), they are good for you! And what an easy way to eat five servings of fruits and vegetables every day. Make sure your salad greens are fresh and carefully washed.

Greek Spinach Salad

• PAMELA AND ERMA WILLIAMS

- 1 3-ounce package sun-dried tomatoes
- 1 cup boiling water
- 1 cucumber
- 8 cups torn fresh spinach
- 1 small red onion, thinly sliced
- 1 cup sliced mushrooms
  Parmesan cheese

DRESSING:

- ½ cup olive oil
- ¼ cup lemon juice
  Salt to taste

Salad: Place tomatoes in a small bowl and add boiling water. Let set for 10 minutes. Drain and set aside. Cut cucumber in half lengthwise, and scoop out seeds. Cut cucumber into thin slices. Combine tomatoes, cucumber, and the next four ingredients. Toss with dressing and serve. *Dressing:* Combine all ingredients in a covered jar and shake jar vigorously to blend.
Makes 8 servings. 170 calories, 13.6 g fat.

Summer Salad Bowl

• PAT HUMPHREY

- 1 medium head Boston lettuce
- ½ pound spinach
- 1 bunch watercress
- ¼ cup zucchini, thinly sliced
- 2 cucumbers, chopped
- 1 onion, cut into rings
- 1 cup celery, chopped
- ½ cup Sprouts Dressing (follows)

Blend dressing ingredients and chill. Tear lettuce and spinach into bite-size pieces. Break watercress, discarding coarse stems. Place greens into bowl and add remaining vegetable. Pour dressing over salad and toss. Chill before serving.
Makes 8 servings. 28 calories, 0 g fat, 64 mg sodium.

Sprouts Dressing

• PAT HUMPHREY

- ½ cup alfalfa sprouts
- 1 teaspoon celery salt
- ½ cup oil
- 1 tablespoon honey
- 2 tablespoons lemon juice
- ½ teaspoon onion powder
- 1 tablespoon sesame seeds

Makes 6 servings. 144 calories, 15 g fat, 128 mg sodium.

Watercress Salad (Barbados)

• PAT HUMPHREY

- 1 bunch watercress
- 1 head Boston lettuce
- ¼ cup olive oil
- 2 tablespoons lime juice
- ½ teaspoon maple syrup
- ½ teaspoon ground cumin
- 1 teaspoon tamari soy sauce
- 1 clove garlic, minced
- 1 small red onion

Discard tough watercress stems. Cut up leaves and tender sprigs. Cut or tear lettuce into small pieces. Combine in bowl. Combine remaining ingredients (except onion) in small jar with tight-fitting lid. Shake vigorously and toss dressing onto salad. Cut onion into thin rings and arrange on top of greens.
Makes 4 servings. 160 calories, 14 g fat, 96 mg sodium.

Mixed Greens and Watercress Salad

• PAMELA AND ERMA WILLIAMS

- ½ head Boston lettuce, rinsed and torn
- ½ head red leaf lettuce, rinsed and torn
- 1 bunch watercress, rinsed and torn

DRESSING

- 1 tablespoon lemon juice
- ⅛ teaspoon salt
- 1-2 cloves of minced garlic
- 2 tablespoons oil

Combine lettuce and watercress in a bowl. Set aside. Combine dressing ingredients in a covered jar and shake to blend. Pour over greens. Toss.
Makes 6 servings. 78 calories, 4.5 g fat.

Caesar Salad

• ERMA WILLIAMS

- 2 heads of romaine lettuce, torn into bite-size pieces
- 1 cup Garlic-flavored Croutons (recipe below) Parmesan cheese

DRESSING

- 2 cloves garlic, chopped
- 3 tablespoons olive oil
- 2 tablespoons lemon juice
- 2 teaspoons Tamari soy sauce
- 8 black olives, finely chopped into paste

Dressing: Soak the garlic in the olive oil for 30 minutes or longer. Remove garlic and discard. In a jar, mix the olive oil, lemon juice, soy sauce, and olive paste. Cover with lid and shake until mixture is blended. Place lettuce in a large bowl and toss with dressing. Sprinkle with croutons and parmesan cheese and serve.
Makes 6 serving. 100 calories, 8 g fat.

Garlic-Flavored Croutons

• ERMA WILLIAMS

- 2 slices whole wheat bread
- 2 teaspoons oil
  Paprika
  Garlic powder
  Salt

Preheat oven to 300° F. Cut bread into 1-inch cubes. Heat oil in a shallow pan. Add cubes and toss lightly. Sprinkle with paprika, garlic powder, and salt. Bake for 20 minutes in oven or until brown.
Makes 4 serving. 46 calories, 1.9 g fat.

Caesar Salad

• JOCELYN M. PETERSON

- ½ head lettuce
- ½ bunch romaine lettuce
- ½ head endive
- 12 radishes, sliced thin
- 2 green onions, sliced
- 1 cup garlic croutons
- 4 tablespoons French dressing

Mix together and top with dressing. Add croutons.
Makes 6 servings. 120 calories, 2 g fat, 50 mg sodium.

Fresh Spinach Salad

• JOCELYN M. PETERSON

- ½ pound fresh spinach, cut in shreds
- 1 medium onion, minced
- 4 tablespoons diced celery
- ¼ cup scrambled tofu
- ½ teaspoon McKay's Chicken Style Seasoning

Toss and chill salad. Add dressing of choice.
Makes 8 serving. 100 calories, 1 g fat, 50 mg sodium.

Chef Salad With Tofu Bits

• JOCELYN M. PETERSON

- 4 cups bite-sized lettuce
- 2 medium tomatoes, chopped
- ½ cup sweet peppers, chopped
- ¼ cup olives
- ½ cup chickpeas (canned)
- ½ cup tofu bits

Mix all ingredients. Add salad dressing of choice.
Makes 6 servings. 80 calories, trace fat, trace sodium.

Party Coleslaw

• JOCELYN M. PETERSON

    1 medium head cabbage, shredded
    2 cups seedless grapes
    ¼ cup slivered almonds
    1 teaspoon honey
    2 tablespoons lemon juice
    1 teaspoon grated onion (optional)
    1 teaspoon McKay's Chicken Style Seasoning
    2 tablespoons soy mayonnaise

Mix cabbage, grapes, and almonds lightly. Beat together honey, lemon juice, onion, seasoning, and soy mayonnaise. Combine all ingredients and serve chilled.
Makes 12 servings. 150 calories, 3 g fat, 100 mg sodium.

Almond Green Bean Salad

• JOCELYN M. PETERSON

    2 cups shredded cooked green beans
    1 tablespoon chopped or sliced pimento
    ¼ cup slivered almonds
    ¼ cup chopped ripe olives
    ¼ cup chopped celery
    1 tablespoon grated onion
    3 tablespoons French dressing
    4 lettuce cups

Toss first six ingredients together with dressing. Serve in lettuce cups.
Makes 4 servings. 260 calories, 4 g fat, 175 mg sodium.

Three-Bean Salad

• JOCELYN M. PETERSON

    1 can garbanzos (chickpeas)
    1 can red kidney beans
    1 cup yellow wax beans
    ¾ cup lemon juice
    ¼ cup corn oil
    ¼ cup honey

    1 large sliced onion
    1 medium sliced green pepper
    1 2-ounce jar pimento
    1 teaspoon Vegit seasoning

Drain beans and combine them in a large container or jar with a tight-fitting lid. To make marinade, blend lemon juice, corn oil, and honey. Pour the marinade into a container that has a tight-fitting lid. Add onion, green pepper, pimento, and seasoning to marinade, cover, shake well, and then pour marinade over bean mixture. Cover bean container and shake to mix well.
Makes 10 servings. 157 calories, 3.7 g fat, 180 mg sodium.

Marinated Garbanzo Salad

• JOCELYN M. PETERSON

    2 cups garbanzo beans, drained
    1 medium onion, chopped
    ½ cup red bell peppers
    2 tablespoons olive oil
    3 tablespoons lemon juice
    ½ teaspoon McKay's Chicken Style Seasoning

Mix all ingredients together. Marinate for one hour. Serve on crisp lettuce leaves.
Makes 6 serving. 180 calories, 4 g fat, 60 mg sodium.

Garbanzo Salad

• PAT HUMPHREY

    2 cups garbanzos
    1 stalk celery, finely chopped
    ¼ cup parsley, chopped
    ¼ cup pimento, chopped
    ½ cup onion, minced
    ½ teaspoon salt
    ½ teaspoon savory

Mix first seven ingredients and serve with Soy Avocado Dressing (recipe next page).
Makes 4 servings. 49 calories, 2.1 g fat, 293 mg sodium.

Soy Avocado Dressing
• PAT HUMPHREY

- 1 cup water
- ½ cup soy milk powder
- 1 large avocado
- ⅓ cup lemon juice
- 1 teaspoon salt
- 1 teaspoon onion powder
- ½ teaspoon dill

Blend water and soy milk powder. Add avocado and blend until smooth and creamy. Remove from blender and fold in ⅓ cup lemon juice. Add salt, onion powder, dill, and other seasonings to taste. Makes 1½ cups (2 tablespoons per serving). 40 calories, 2.3 g fat, 128 mg sodium.

Cucumber, Avocado, and Red Onion Salad
• DONNA A. SMITH

- 2 medium cucumbers
- 1 avocado, sliced
- 1 medium red onion
- ½ teaspoon salt
- ½ cup Nayonnaise
- 1 tablespoon lemon juice
- 1 tablespoon brown sugar
- 1 teaspoon dried dillweed
- ¼ teaspoon cayenne pepper

Toss cucumbers, avocado, and red onions. Combine salt, Nayonnaise, lemon juice, brown sugar, dill weed, and cayenne pepper in medium bowl. Combine everything, chill, and serve. Makes 6 servings. 116 calories, 9 g fat, 322 mg sodium.

COOK'S HINT: Meatloaf Sauce from p. 91 may also be used as a salad dressing.

Italian-Style Cauliflower Salad
• PAT HUMPHREY

- 1 head cauliflower, cut into florets
- 1 cup sliced green or red bell pepper
- 1 cup sliced celery
- 1 cup sliced carrots
- ½ cup pimento-stuffed olives, sliced
- ¼ cup parsley, chopped

DRESSING

- ½ cup olive oil
- ¼ cup lemon juice
- 1 clove garlic
- ½ teaspoon salt
- ¼ teaspoon dried basil

Steam cauliflower in steamer basket for about 8 minutes or until crisp-tender. Drain and place in a large bowl. Combine olive oil, lemon juice, garlic, salt, and basil to make dressing. Pour dressing over warm cauliflower, then add remaining ingredients. Toss to coat. Cover and refrigerate several hours before serving. Makes 6 serving. 230 calories, 19 g fat, 282 mg sodium.

HEALTHY OPTION: Reduce or omit oil for low-fat diets.

Broccoli and Cauliflower Florets Salad

• ERMA WILLIAMS

½ pound broccoli florets
½ pound cauliflower florets
3 sun-dried tomatoes, soaked in hot water
1 tablespoon toasted pine nuts

DRESSING

1 small garlic, minced
4 tablespoons olive oil
2 tablespoons lemon juice
Salt and cayenne pepper to taste

Dressing: In a small bowl whisk garlic, olive oil, lemon juice, salt, and cayenne pepper. Set aside Salad: Cut florets into bite-size pieces. Place florets into a medium pot of boiling water. Cook for about 2 minutes or until florets are slightly crisp and bright in color. Drain. Chop sun-dried tomatoes into small pieces and toss with florets, pine nuts, and olive oil dressing.
Makes 4 servings. 112 calories, 8 g fat.

Cauliflower Salad

• PAT HUMPHREY

1 medium head
Cauliflower, sliced thin
¼ green onion, minced
½ cup celery, chopped

Combine cauliflower, onion, and celery in bowl. Toss with French Dressing (recipe below).
Makes 6 servings. 92 calories, 0 g fat, 14 mg sodium.

French Dressing

• PAT HUMPHREY

½ cup oil
¼ cup lemon juice
2 tablespoons honey
2 Roma tomatoes, chopped
1 teaspoon salt

¼ teaspoon onion powder
¼ teaspoon garlic powder

Blend all ingredients thoroughly. Chill.
Serving: 2 tablespoons. 71 calories, 7 g fat, 276 mg sodium

Broccoli Salad

• JOCELYN M. PETERSON

2 tablespoons olive oil
2 tablespoons lemon juice
1 garlic clove, minced
½ teaspoon McKay's Chicken Style Seasoning
½ cup stripped red bell peppers
1 pound cooked broccoli

Mix all ingredients except broccoli, and sprinkle on chilled broccoli.
Makes 6 servings. 85 calories. 2 g fat, 50 mg sodium.

Warm Tofu Salad

• PAMELA WILLIAMS

1 tablespoon olive oil
3 tablespoons lemon juice
2 tablespoons low-sodium soy sauce
½ teaspoon oregano
½ teaspoon basil
1 garlic clove, sliced
1 pound extra firm tofu, drained and cubed
¾ pound spinach, drained
1 large red onion, thinly sliced
1 large yellow bell pepper, sliced
1 cup toasted bread, cubed, sprinkled with Garlic powder

In a small bowl, mix olive oil, lemon juice, soy sauce, oregano, basil, and garlic. Add tofu and marinate for 2 hours. Shred spinach and put into a large bowl. Add the onion, yellow, bell pepper, and toasted bread cubes and mix. Put marinated tofu mixture into a frying pan and place on low heat for 4 minutes, stirring constantly. Stir in the remaining ingredients. Cover and cook for

3 minutes, stirring occasionally. Empty into a bowl, toss and serve immediately.
Makes 4 servings. 165 calories, 8 g fat, 396 mg sodium.

Red and Gold Salad
• JOCELYN PETERSON

- 1 cup grated raw carrots
- 1 cup shredded cabbage
- ¼ cup chopped green onions
- ½ cup grated radish
- ⅓ cup chopped parsley
- ⅓ cup slivered pimento
- ¼ cup soy mayonnaise
- 6 lettuce leaves

Mix vegetables and blend with soy mayonnaise. Serve on lettuce cups.
Makes 6 servings. 200 calories, 5 g fat, 80 mg sodium.

Moroccan Carrot Salad (North African)
• PAMELA WILLIAMS

- 10-12 carrots, peeled and coarsely grated
- ½ cup orange segments
- 1 large white onion, thinly sliced
- ¾ cup radishes, thinly sliced
- ½ cup cilantro, coarsely chopped
- 2 tablespoons olive oil
- 2 tablespoons lemon juice
- 2 tablespoons orange juice
- ⅛ teaspoon grated orange peel
- ½ teaspoon cinnamon
- ⅛ teaspoon salt
- Pita bread

Combine carrots, oranges, radishes, and cilantro in a bowl. Whisk together the olive oil, lemon juice, orange juice, orange peel, cinnamon, and salt. Pour over the salad. Cover and chill. Cut pita bread into wedges. Serve salad with pita wedges.
Makes 6 servings. 169 calories, 5 g fat, 91 mg sodium

Carrot and Apple Salad
• JOCELYN M. PETERSON

- 1 cup grated carrots
- ½ cup diced pineapples packed in juice, drained
- ½ cup diced red Delicious apples
- 1 teaspoon soy mayonnaise
- 1 tablespoon walnuts, chopped

Mix all ingredients well. Chill before serving.
Makes 4 servings. 80 calories, 3 g fat, 10 mg sodium.

Carrot-Coconut Salad
• PAT HUMPHREY

- 3 cups finely shredded carrots
- 1 cup coconut
- ¼ tofu mayonnaise (recipe below)

Mix carrots and coconut. Add mayonnaise and salt to taste.
Makes 8 servings. 85 calories, 7 g fat, 87 mg sodium.

Tofu Mayonnaise 3
• PAT HUMPHREY

- 1 pound tofu, rinsed and drained
- ¼ cup water
- 2 teaspoons salt
- 2 tablespoons honey
- 1 teaspoon onion powder
- ⅓ cup lemon juice
- ⅓ cup raw cashews

Blend tofu with water until liquefied. Add remaining ingredients and blend till creamy.
Makes 10 servings. 70 calories, 4 g fat, 404 mg sodium.

Tofu Mayonnaise 4

• PAT HUMPHREY

   1 10-ounce box firm silken tofu
   3 tablespoons lemon juice
  ½ teaspoon garlic powder
  ¼ cup sunflower seeds
   1 teaspoon onion powder
   1 teaspoon salt

Blend all ingredients, adding just enough water to allow mixture to blend to a smooth consistency.
Makes 20 servings. 19 calories, 1.3 g fat, 101 mg sodium.

Mock Tuna Salad

• PAT HUMPHREY

   1 15-ounce can chickpeas, drained
  ¼ cup PA's pickle relish
  ¼ cup mayonnaise
  ¼ cup purple onion, chopped
   1 stalk celery, chopped
   1 teaspoon soy sauce
  ¼ teaspoon Vege-Sal
   2 tablespoons nutritional yeast flakes

Mix all ingredients, mashing chickpeas lightly. Chill overnight to allow flavors to blend.
Makes 4 servings. 396 calories, 10 g fat, 313 mg sodium.

Tempeh Salad (Orient)

• PAMELA WILLIAMS

   8 ounces tempeh
   1 cup garbanzo beans, cooked and slightly mashed
  ¼ cup liquid from garbanzo beans
   1 tablespoon low-sodium soy sauce
   1 tablespoon lemon juice
  ½ teaspoon garlic, minced
  ¼ teaspoon fresh basil
  ½ teaspoon fresh marjoram
   2 tablespoons onion, minced
   1 tablespoon parsley, minced

  ¼ cup cucumber, chopped
   3 tablespoons soy mayonnaise (recipe below)

Cut tempeh into 2-inch cubes. Spray a medium frying pan with vegetable cooking spray and place over a medium heat. Sauté tempeh for 2 minutes. Remove from heat and cool. In a bowl, mix tempeh with the rest of the ingredients. Chill. Serve as a salad or in a sandwich.
Makes 4 servings. 169 calories, 12.75 g fat, 294 mg sodium.

Soy Mayonnaise 2

   1 cup water
  ¾ teaspoon salt
  ½ teaspoon garlic
  ½ teaspoon onion powder
  ½ cup fresh lemon juice
  ½ cup soy flour
  ½ cup soy protein powder
 1½ cups soy oil
  ½ cup canola oil

Blend salt, garlic, onion, lemon juice, flour, protein powder, water, and ½ cup of the oil until well mixed. Turn the blender to the lowest speed and blend the mixture. Slowly add the remaining oil while blender is still on low speed. Blend until the mixture is smooth and thick. Chill.
Makes about 2 cups (32 servings). 129 calories, 13.5 g fat, 29 mg sodium.

Gazpacho Salad

• PAT HUMPHREY

   1 cup cucumbers, diced
  ¼ cup tomatoes, diced
   1 cup bell peppers, diced
  ⅛ cup green onions, chopped

Dressing

   1 teaspoon olive oil
 1½ tablespoon lemon juice
  ½ teaspoon salt
   2 teaspoons fresh parsley, minced
  ¼ teaspoon garlic powder

Combine vegetables in a bowl. Mix dressing ingredients and stir into vegetables. Chill.
Makes 6 servings. 31 calories, 1 g fat, 176 mg sodium.

Eggplant Caviar
• ERMA WILLIAMS

   2 medium eggplants
   6 garlic cloves, unpeeled
   3 tablespoons olive oil
   3 sun-dried tomatoes, soaked in hot water and chopped
   2 teaspoons lemon juice
   1 tablespoon red grape juice
      salt and cayenne pepper to taste

Preheat oven to 375° F. Cut eggplant in half. Brush sheet with olive oil and place eggplant face down. Place unpeeled garlic on same sheet with the eggplant. Bake for 30 minutes or until eggplant is tender. Cool. Peel skin from eggplant and chop. Peel garlic and chop. Place eggplant in food processor and chop. Toss with olive oil, sun-dried tomatoes, garlic, lemon juice, grape juice, salt and cayenne pepper. Set aside for an hour. Serve. Optional: garnish with Italian parsley.
Makes 4 serving. 173 calories, 10 g fat.

Artichoke Pasta Salad
• JOCELYN M. PETERSON ·

   2 cups cooked macaroni
   1 6-ounce jar artichoke hearts
   4 ounces fresh small mushroom, sliced
   2 medium tomatoes, sliced
   1 cup grated carrots
  ¼ cup medium pitted olives
   1 teaspoon McKay's Chicken Style Seasoning

Mix all ingredients together. Chill for one hour before serving.
Makes 6 servings. 280 calories, 5 g fat, 150 mg sodium.

Vegetable Medley Salad
• ERMA WILLIAMS

   1 head of red leaf lettuce
   1 cup cooked red potatoes, unpeeled and cubed
   1 cup cooked carrots, cubed
   1 cup cooked string beans
  ¼ cup green peppers, cut into small squares
  ¼ cup scallions cut into 2-inch strips
      French Dressing (p. 64, 69)
      Paprika
      Sprigs of parsley

Wash and arrange lettuce leaves. Toss vegetables with French Dressing and seasonings. Place on lettuce leaves. Garnish with paprika and sprigs of parsley.
Makes 4 servings. 85 calories, 0 g fat.

Macaroni Club Salad
• JOCELYN M. PETERSON

   2 cups cooked elbow macaroni, drained
  ¼ cup minced ripe olives
  ½ cup diced celery
   1 tablespoon minced onion
   1 tablespoon minced green peppers
   1 teaspoon of McKay's Chicken Style Seasoning
   2 tablespoons soy mayonnaise
   2 tablespoons lemon juice
   1 cup cooked peas
   6 lettuce cups

Combine all ingredients except the last four. Blend soy mayonnaise with lemon juice and add to macaroni mixture; mix well. Add peas and toss lightly. Serve on lettuce cups.
Makes 6 servings. 180 calories, 4 g fat, 200 mg sodium.

Caribbean Potato Salad
• JOCELYN M. PETERSON

  1 chopped onion
  ½ cup chopped red bell pepper
  2 tablespoons olive oil
  1 tablespoon cumin
  1 tablespoon dried parsley
  1 tablespoon sweet basil
  1 teaspoon Vegit Seasoning
  1 teaspoon garlic powder
  1 8-ounce package frozen peas and carrots
  3 pounds white cooked potatoes, diced and cooled
  2 tablespoons sweet pickle relish
  2 tablespoons soy mayonnaise

Sauté onions and red bell pepper in olive oil. Add seasonings and peas and carrots. Simmer and let cool. Add to cooled potatoes and add salad dressing and sweet pickle relish. Refrigerate before serving.
Makes 12 servings. 250 calories, 5 g fat, 120 mg sodium.

Potato Salad
• PAT HUMPHREY

  6 cups cooked potatoes, diced
  2 tablespoons onion powder
  ⅛ teaspoon garlic powder
  1 onion, chopped
  2 cups black olives, chopped
  2 cups avocado, cubed
  ¼ cup PA's Pickle Relish
  ½ teaspoon celery salt
  ½ teaspoon dillweed
1½ teaspoons salt
    Tofu Mayonnaise (recipe below)
    Paprika
    Chopped parsley

Mix first eight ingredients, then add enough mayonnaise to moisten. Sprinkle with paprika and garnish with parsley.
Makes 12 servings. 218 calories, 16 g fat, 1,064 mg sodium.

Tofu Mayonnaise 5
• PAT HUMPHREY

  1 10.5-ounce package tofu
  ⅛ cup water
  ½ teaspoon salt
  ⅛ teaspoon garlic powder
  1 teaspoon onion powder
  ⅛ teaspoon basil
  3 tablespoons honey
  ⅓ cup lemon juice
  ⅓ cup raw cashews, rinsed

Blend all ingredients except tofu. When smooth, add tofu and blend. Chill.
Makes 6 servings. 42 calories, 2.5 g fat, 51 mg sodium.

Creamy Coleslaw
• PAT HUMPHREY

  2 cups green cabbage, shredded
  2 cups red cabbage, shredded
  1 cup celery, coarsely chopped
  1 red bell pepper, cut in ½-in pieces

Place all ingredients in a non-metallic bowl and toss. Add ½ cup Cashew Dressing (recipe below). Mix well, cover, and chill for several hours.
Makes 4 servings. 60 calories (without dressing), 1 g fat, 22 mg sodium.

Cashew Dressing
• PAT HUMPHREY

  2 cups sweet orange juice
  8 ounces cashew butter

Blend orange juice and cashew until smooth. Add more or less orange juice to achieve desired consistency.
Makes 24 servings (2 tablespoons each). 75 calories, 4.6 g fat, 6.5 mg sodium.

DRESSINGS

Basil Dressing
• ERMA WILLIAMS

- 5 ounces silken tofu
- 2 tablespoons lemon juice
- 2 tablespoons apple juice
- 2 tablespoons orange juice
- 1 clove garlic, minced
- 2 tablespoons fresh chopped basil
  Salt

Blend all ingredients in a blender or food processor. Blend until smooth. Refrigerate.
Makes 6 servings. 46 calories, 1.9 g fat.

Fresh Tomato Dressing
• ERMA WILLIAMS

- ½ cup chopped Roma tomatoes
- 2 tablespoons lemon juice
- 1 tablespoon chopped onion
- ¼ teaspoon paprika
- 1 small clove garlic, chopped
- ½ teaspoon chopped parsley

Place all ingredients, except parsley, in a blender. Blend until smooth. Add chopped parsley and serve on salad.
Makes 2 servings. 17 calories, 0 g fat.

Quick French Dressing
• ERMA WILLIAMS

- ½ cup tomato juice
- 2 tablespoons lemon juice
- 1 tablespoon finely chopped onion
- ½ teaspoon sugar
- ¼ teaspoon salt

Combine all ingredients in a jar. Cover and shake just before serving.
Makes 6 servings. 13 calories, 0 g fat.

French Dressing
• DONNA GREEN GOODMAN

- 1 cup soy, corn, safflower, or canola oil
- ⅓ cup fresh lemon juice
- ⅓ cup honey
- ½ tablespoon paprika
- ¾ cup tomato puree
- ½ tablespoon onion powder
- 1 teaspoon garlic powder
- 1 teaspoon salt

Blend all ingredients on the stove top on high for 30 seconds. Chill in covered container.
Makes 2½ cups (2 tablespoons per serving).
58 calories, 5 g fat, 60 mg sodium.

Herbal Lemon Dressing
• JOCELYN M. PETERSON

- ½ cup olive oil
- ¼ cup lemon juice
- 2 teaspoons herb seasonings, as desired
- ¼ teaspoon garlic powder
- ¼ teaspoon grated onion
- ¼ teaspoon parsley
- ¼ teaspoon basil

Mix all ingredients together well. Store in refrigerator.
Makes 8-10 servings (2 tablespoons per serving).
80 calories, 3 g fat, 0 mg sodium.

Italian Dressing
• PAT HUMPHREY

- ⅓ cup olive oil
- 2 tablespoons lemon juice
- 1 garlic clove, pressed
- 1 tablespoon fresh parsley, chopped
- ½ teaspoon salt

Mix all ingredients together.
Makes 6 servings. 69 calories, 13 g fat, 188 mg sodium.

FRUIT SALADS

Waldorf Salad
• JOHNETTA FRAZIER

    4 cups apples, cored and chopped (red, yellow, and green)
  1½ cups mandarin orange segments
   ⅔ cups raisins
   ⅓ cup walnuts, chopped
   ½ cup orange juice, freshly squeezed
   ½ cup lemon juice, freshly squeezed
    2 tablespoons honey

Combine apples, orange segments, raisins, and walnuts in bowl. Mix juices and honey together and pour over fruit and nut mixture. Chill.
Makes 8 servings. 127 calories, 3 g fat, 2 mg sodium.

Waldorf Salad With Nayonaise
• DONNA A. SMITH
   ¼ cup Nayonnaise
    2 teaspoons unsweetened pineapple juice
   ½ cup yogurt with fruit of your choice (if not moist enough, use more yogurt)
    3 small red apples, diced
   ½ cup celery, diced
   ¼ cup walnuts, chopped
   ⅓ cup pineapple tidbits
   ¼ cup raisins

Mix Nayonnaise, pineapple juice, and yogurt. Add apples, celery, walnuts, pineapple tidbits, and raisins.
Makes 6 servings. 506 calories, 6 g fat, 118 mg sodium.

Fruited Chicken-Style Salad With Pecans
• JOHNETTA FRAZIER
    2 cups chopped soy chicken
   ¼ cup soy mayonnaise
    1 tablespoon lemon juice
    1 teaspoon honey

    1 teaspoon McKay's Chicken Style Seasoning
  1½ cup seedless grapes
   ½ cup chopped celery
   ¼ cup red onions, chopped
   ¼ cup chopped pecans
    6 Boston lettuce leaves

Mix all ingredients together. Chill and serve on Boston lettuce leaves.
Makes 6 servings. 250 calories, 5 g fat, 100 mg sodium.

Cashew Nut Apple Salad
• JOCELYN M. PETERSON
   ¼ cup soy mayonnaise
    2 tablespoons chopped cashew nuts
   ½ cup diced apple
    1 cup diced soyameat (or Scallops, or other gluten preparation)
   ½ cup diced celery
    2 tablespoons chopped green onion
   ½ tablespoon McKay's Chicken Style Seasoning
    6 lettuce leaves

Mix soy mayonnaise and cashew nuts; chill. Combine remaining ingredients; serve on lettuce.
Makes 4 servings. 250 calories, 3 g fat, 150 mg sodium.

Nutty Fruity Salad
• JOHNETTA FRAZIER
    6 apples, cored and sliced
      Lemon juice
    1 cup raisins
   ½ cup chopped walnuts
    1 cup white grape juice
    2 dates, pitted and chopped
   ⅛ teaspoon salt
    2 tablespoons peanuts, chopped

Pour a splash of lemon juice over apple slices. Combine apples and raisins in bowl. Place walnuts,

white grape juice, dates, and salt in blender and mix until smooth. Pour walnut cream mixture over fruit and chill. Sprinkle peanuts over salad before serving.
Makes 8 servings. 171 calories, 6 g fat, 39 mg sodium.

Cranberry-Walnut Salad
• JOHNETTA FRAZIER

    4 tablespoons kosher plain gelatin
    2½ cups boiling water
    12 ounces cranberry apple juice concentrate
    1 cup water
    2 cups cranberries
    2 apples, cored and quartered
    1 orange, peeled, seeded, and quartered
    ⅔ cup chopped walnuts

Place gelatin in boiling water. Add cranberry apple juice and water. Chill. Chop cranberries, apples, and orange in food processor. When gelatin mixture begins to thicken, add chopped fruits and nuts and then pour into mold.
Makes 15 servings. 106 calories, 3 g fat, 14 mg sodium.

Caribbean Fruit Salad
• ERMA WILLIAMS

    1 banana, sliced
    ½ cantaloupe, cubed
    1 apple, cubed
    2 kiwis, sliced (if available)
    1 8-ounce can or fresh pineapple, cut into chunks

Prepare dressing (recipe below) and set aside. Place cut fruit into a large bowl. Spoon dressing on fruit. Refrigerate and serve chilled. *Optional:* garnish with shredded coconut.
Dressing:

    ½ teaspoon fresh grated ginger
    1 tablespoon honey
    1 lemon (juice)

    1 lime (juice)

In a small bowl, mix ginger and honey. Add lemon and lime juice gradually and stir. Set aside.
Makes 4 servings: 101 calories, 0 g fat.

Tropical Fruit Salad
• PAMELA WILLIAMS

    2 firm ripe bananas
    ½ teaspoon fresh lemon juice
    1 ripe papaya
    2 ripe mangoes
    1 ripe pineapple
    Shredded coconut

Peel and cut bananas into 2-inch slices and place in a bowl. Cover bananas with lemon juice to keep them from turning brown. Peel and cut papaya, mango, and pineapple into chunks and mix with bananas. Sprinkle a small amount of coconut on the mixture of fruit. Stir and chill before serving.
Makes 4 servings. 162 calories, 0 g fat, 5 mg sodium.

Hawaiian Salad
• JOCELYN M. PETERSON

    6 pineapple slices (fresh or canned)
    1 mango, diced
    ½ cup papaya, diced
    ½ cantaloupe, diced
    1 large orange, chopped
    2 tablespoons maple syrup or honey
    ⅓ cup fresh orange juice
    ¼ cup chopped mint leaves
    Lettuce leaves

Mix all ingredients except lettuce. Chill for 15 minutes. Serve on lettuce leaves.
Makes 6 servings. 120 calories, 0 g fat, trace sodium.

Tropical Delight
• ERMA WILLIAMS

   1 papaya, cubed
   1 mango, cubed
   1 banana, sliced
  10 cherries, pitted and sliced
   1 can pineapple chunks, drained
  ½ lemon, cubed
   1 teaspoon chopped mint
   2 tablespoons walnuts, chopped

Combine all ingredients in a salad bowl. Toss and chill.
Makes 4 servings. 140 calories, 1.5 g fat.

Mango-Papaya Salad
• JOHNETTA FRAZIER

  2 papayas, peeled, seeded and cut in large pieces
  2 mangoes, peeled, seeded and cut in large pieces
  2 limes

Combine fruit and juice of one lime. Chill. Serve with sliced lime as garnish.
Makes 4 servings. 132 calories, 1 g fat, 7 mg sodium.

Papaya Salad
• PAMELA AND ERMA WILLIAMS

  2 cups of firm ripe papaya, peeled, seeded, and cubed
  1 cup fresh pineapple chunks
  1 cup tangerine segments, remove seeds
  1 large ripe banana, peeled and cut into slices
  1 tablespoon fresh lemon juice
  ¼ cup shredded coconut
     Artificial sweetener

Combine all ingredients in a bowl. Sprinkle with lemon juice and a touch of sweetener, if needed. Chill and serve topped with coconut.
Makes 4 servings. 120 calories, 2 g fat, 6 mg sodium.

Layered Melon Ball Fruit Salad
• JOHNETTA FRAZIER

  2 cups watermelon, scooped into balls
  2 cups honeydew, scooped into balls
  2 cups cantaloupe, scooped into balls

Place fruit in glass bowl. Layer fruit as listed above and chill. Garnish on top with a sprig of mint and a few blueberries or raspberries.
Makes 6 servings. 62 calories, 0 g fat, 11 mg sodium.

Nectarine-Raspberry Fruit Salad
• JOHNETTA FRAZIER

  6 nectarines, sliced
  2 cups raspberries
  ¼ cup fresh orange juice
  ½ cup apple juice concentrate
  ¾ cup water
  6 raspberries

Combine first three ingredients. Blend apple juice concentrate, water, and raspberries. Spoon fruit into separate bowls and drizzle with juice mixture.
Makes 8 servings. 100 calories, 0 g fat, 4 mg sodium.

Honey-Yogurt Fruit Salad
• JOHNETTA FRAZIER

  1½ cups pineapple chunks
  3 bananas, sliced
  2 oranges, peeled and sliced
  1 cup red seedless grapes
  6 ounces Silk soy plain yogurt
  3 tablespoons honey
  1 teaspoon vanilla extract

Mix fruit in bowl. Blend yogurt, honey, and vanilla and add to fruit mixture, chill.
Makes 10 servings. 102 calories, 0 g fat, 2 mg sodium.

Salads and Dressing

Ambrosia Salad

• DONNA A. SMITH

- ½ cup tropical fruit salad
- 1 cup canned mandarin oranges, drained
- 1 small banana, sliced
- ½ cup nondairy whipped topping
- ¼ cup juice tropical fruit salad
- 2 tablespoons shredded coconut

Mix tropical fruit salad, mandarin oranges, and bananas and fold in whipped topping and juice from tropical fruit salad. Top with shredded coconut and chill before serving.

Makes 4 servings. 129 calories, 4 g fat, 11 mg sodium.

Ambrosia Salad (Soy Yogurt)

• JOHNETTA FRAZIER

- 1 cup red seedless grapes
- 3 bananas, sliced
- 2 cups mandarin orange segments
- 2 cups pineapple chunks
- ½ cup unsweetened coconut
- 12 ounces Silk plain soy yogurt
- 4 tablespoons honey
- 1 teaspoon clear vanilla extract

Mix fruit and coconut in bowl. Blend yogurt, honey, and vanilla extract. Stir yogurt mixture into fruit mix, chill. Sprinkle a tablespoon of coconut on top before serving.

Makes 10 servings. 168 calories, 3 g fat, 9 mg sodium.

Creamy Tofu Ambrosia Salad

• JOCELYN M. PETERSON

- ¾ cup diced orange sections
- 2 bananas, sliced
- ¼ cup green seedless grapes
- 3 tablespoons lemon juice (sprinkle over fruit)
- 4 ounces silken tofu (whipped with 1 teaspoon of honey)
- 2 tablespoons grated coconut (optional)

Mix all ingredients together.

Makes 4 servings. 80 calories, 2 g fat, 50 mg sodium.

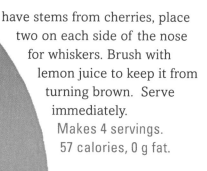

have stems from cherries, place two on each side of the nose for whiskers. Brush with lemon juice to keep it from turning brown. Serve immediately.
Makes 4 servings.
57 calories, 0 g fat.

Banana-Strawberry Salad

• JOHNETTA FRAZIER

- 1 tablespoon lemon juice
- 2 bananas, sliced
- 2 cups strawberries, hulled and halved
- ½ cup strawberry juice concentrate
- ½ cup water
- 6 strawberries

Combine lemon juice and sliced bananas in bowl. Add strawberries. Blend concentrate, water, and six strawberries. Pour over mixed fruit and chill. Serve with a dollop of banana cream.
Makes 6 servings. 98 calories, 2 g fat, 5 mg sodium.

Fun 'n' Fruity Salad (Kids)

• PAMELA AND ERMA WILLIAMS

- 1 pear, peeled, cored, and cut in half
- 4 canned prunes, pitted, and cut in half
- 8 raisins
- 4 cherries, pitted, and cut in half
- 1 apple, peeled, cored, and cut in half
  Lemon juice

PUPPY DOG: Place pear half face down on a salad plate. Place one half of prune on each side of the broad portion of the pear for ears. Place two raisins in the middle of the pear for eyes. Then on the narrow tip of the pear, place a half of a cherry for its nose. Brush with lemon juice to keep it from turning brown. Serve immediately. KITTY CAT: Place apple half face down on a salad plate. Place two raisins in the middle for eyes with an inch between them. Place half of a cherry to make a nose. If you

Fruit Salad

• DONNA GREEN GOODMAN

- 1 can unsweetened crushed pineapple in its own juice
- 1 can whole-berry cranberry sauce or plain cranberry sauce
- 2 cups frozen, unsweetened strawberries, sliced
- 1 cup frozen, unsweetened blueberries
- 1 cup chopped pecans

Mix all ingredients. Allow to chill thoroughly before serving.
Makes 10 servings. 146 calories, 4 g fat, 13 mg sodium.
SERVING IDEA: Excellent as a side dish or over bread or cake.

Very Berry Salad

• JOHNETTA FRAZIER

>   2 cups blueberries
>   2 cups strawberries
> 1½ cups raspberries
> 1½ cups blackberries
>   ¾ cups strawberry juice concentrate
> 1½ cups water
>   Kiwi slices

Combine in bowl. Chill for 20 to 30 minutes. Garnish with kiwi slices.

Makes 8 servings: 98 calories, 0 g fat, 6 mg sodium.

Pineapple Fruit Salad

• JOHNETTA FRAZIER

>   1 pineapple
>   2 mangos, peeled and cut in large pieces
> 1½ cups red seedless grapes
>   1 banana, sliced
>   ¼ cup fresh lemon juice

Quarter pineapple lengthwise. Hold pineapple quarter tightly and slice fruit from rind, keeping rind intact. Discard the core. Cut pineapple into chunks and place in bowl with remaining fruit and lemon juice. Allow fruit to chill. Scoop fruit salad into pineapple shells and serve.

Makes 4 servings. 180 calories, 1 g fat, 4 mg sodium.

Fresh Pineapple Salad

• JOCELYN M. PETERSON

>   1 small ripe pineapple
>   1 tablespoon fresh lemon juice
>   ½ cup fresh dates, pitted and quartered
>   8 ounces fresh strawberries, sliced
>   Several fresh mint sprigs, to serve

Cut the skin from the pineapple and, using the tip of a vegetable peeler, remove as many brown "eyes" as possible. Quarter lengthwise, remove the core, then slice, lay the pineapple in a shallow, pretty glass bowl. Sprinkle with lemon juice. Add the dates and strawberries, cover, and chill for 2 hours, stirring once or twice. Serve lightly chilled, garnished with a few mint sprigs.

Makes 4 servings. 60 calories, 0 g fat, 10 mg sodium.

Cranberry Orange Relish

• PAMELA AND ERMA WILLIAMS

>   1 orange (preferably seedless)
>   1 12-ounce package fresh cranberries
>   Honey to taste

Cut whole orange into chunks. Place half the cranberries and half the orange in a food processor. Blend until evenly chopped. Place mixture in a bowl and repeat the process. Stir in honey to taste. Chill or freeze.

Makes 2½ cups (½ cup per serving). 292 calories, 0 g fat.

Citrus Fruit Salad

• JOHNETTA FRAZIER

>   2 lemons
>   2 limes
>   2 oranges
>   ½ cup honey
>   ½ cup water
>   4 oranges, peeled and segmented
>   2 white grapefruits, peeled and segmented
>   2 pink grapefruits, peeled and segmented

Grate one teaspoon each of lemon, lime, and orange rinds. Juice lemons, limes, and oranges. Combine segmented fruit in bowl. Pour syrup over fruit and allow to chill. Garnish with twisted lime slice.

Makes 12 servings. 111 calories, 0 g fat, 2 mg sodium.

Main Dishes

What is tiny, delicious, and packed with ingredients that benefit health? The soybean! Scientists report that soybeans may help reduce the risk of heart disease and cancer. And soybeans supply all the essential amino acids. And if this isn't enough, foods made with soybeans taste great! So if you want more soy in your diet, just add these soy food recipes to your menus. In addition to main dish recipes based on soy, we've also included a wide variety of recipes featuring legumes, nuts, and wheat gluten, which are also good for you! At the end of this section, you'll find delightful recipes for Italian and Mexican cuisine.

SOY AND TOFU

Soybean Casserole
• PAMELA WILLIAMS

    1 cup rice, cooked
    1 cup soybeans, cooked
    ¼ cup onion, chopped
    1 cup mushrooms, chopped
    1 can mushroom soup
    1 12-ounce package Morningstar® Recipe Crumbles
    1 cup soy milk

Combine all ingredients in a casserole dish and bake at 350° F for 30 minutes or until it is heated through to the middle. Garnish with parsley or chopped scallions.
Makes 6 servings. 239 calories, 8.6 g fat, 914 mg sodium.

Tofu Patties
• PAT HUMPHREY

    1 pound tofu
    ¾ cup water
    1 medium onion quartered
    2 cloves garlic
    2 tablespoons soy sauce
    1 teaspoon salt
    ½ teaspoon marjoram
    ¼ teaspoon thyme
    3½ cups oatmeal

Blend all ingredients except oatmeal. Pour mixture into bowl and stir in oatmeal.
Form into patties and bake at 350° F for 30 to 40 minutes, turning once.
Makes 12 servings. 140 calories, 3.6 g fat, 248 mg sodium.

Tofu Loves You!
One 4 ounce serving of tofu packs 18% of an adult's daily requirement for protein, and protein is crucial in building muscle. That same 4 ounce serving also contains one-third of the daily requirement of iron, as well as strong doses of antioxidants manganese, copper and selenium. These nutrients contribute to maintaining energy levels. Anti-oxidants are also believed to help prevent against a myriad of cancers by protecting DNA.

www.essortment.com/lifestyle
/foodinformation_ttwz.htm

Main Dishes

Tofu Patties
• JOCELYN M. PETERSON

- 1½ cups whole grain cereal flakes, crushed
- 1 pound tofu, mashed
- 2 teaspoons cinnamon or coriander
- 2 teaspoons vanilla flavoring
  Nonstick cooking spray
- ¼ cup wheat germ

Combine cereal flakes, tofu, and flavoring. Knead with your hands until thoroughly mixed. Let stand for a few minutes. Spray skillet with nonstick cooking spray. Using ¼ cup at a time, shape tofu mixture into flat 2-inch rounds, coat with wheat germ, and place in hot pan. Brown on each side. Serve with fruit toppings.
Makes 4 servings. 171 calories, 4 g fat, 30 mg sodium.
VARIATION: Omit cinnamon and vanilla; season with 1 tablespoon soy sauce and 1 tablespoon minced onion.

Walnut Broccoli Stir-Fry (Orient)
• JOCELYN M. PETERSON

- 1 pound firm tofu, cut into 1-inch cubes
- 3 tablespoons olive oil
- 1 cup water
- ½ teaspoon Vege-Sal
- 2 carrots, sliced thin
- 2 cups broccoli florets, with 1-or 2 inch stems
- 2 onions, thinly sliced
- 1 cup mushrooms, sliced
- ½ cup walnut halves
- 1 tablespoon cornstarch
- ½ teaspoon cumin
- 3 tablespoons soy sauce (low sodium)

Cut tofu and brown lightly in 2 tablespoons of olive oil. In another pot bring water and Vege-Sal to a boil. Drop carrots and broccoli into boiling water for one minute. Drain and reserve the liquid. In a wok or large frying pan, sauté onions, mushrooms, and walnuts in a tablespoon of olive oil over medium heat until soft. Increase heat to medium high and add the carrots and broccoli. Stir. Add tofu cubes; stir again. To reserved vegetable stock, add cornstarch, cumin, and soy sauce, Pour over the vegetables and tofu, then stir and cook everything until bubbling. Serve hot over rice or Chinese noodles.
Makes 6 servings. 245 calories, 5 g fat, 60 mg sodium.

Tofu Mafe
• PAMELA WILLIAMS

- 1 tablespoon peanut oil
- 1 teaspoon cayenne pepper
- 1 cup onion, chopped
- 1 cup squash, cubed
- 1 cup turnips, cubed
- 1 cup potatoes, cubed
- 1 cup carrots, sliced
- 1 cup cabbage, shredded
- 1 cup tomatoes, blanched, peeled, chopped
- 2 green onions, cut into 1-inch pieces
- 1 cup tomato sauce
- ½ cup water
- ⅓ cup peanut butter
- 2 cups tofu, cubed

In a heavy saucepan add peanut oil and onions. Sauté until onions are tender. Add cayenne pepper and vegetables one at a time and mix well with onions. Add tomato sauce and ½ cup water. Simmer until vegetables are tender but crisp. Remove ½ cup of liquid and mix with peanut butter. Add this mixture to the saucepan and cook for five minutes. Add tofu and cook for an additional 10 minutes. Serve.
Makes 6 servings. 207 calories, 12 g fat, 100 mg sodium.

Spinach Quiche
• CHRISTINA FLEMING-GABRIEL

- 1 tablespoon vegetable oil
- 1 large onion, chopped
- 1 10-ounce package frozen, chopped spinach, or 1½ cup leftover cooked spinach

1¼ cups Egg Beaters (or other egg substitute)
12 ounces Soya Kaas Cheddar cheese
Salt (optional)

Preheat oven to 350° F. In a large frying pan over medium heat, add vegetable oil and onion. Sauté onion until translucent. Stir in spinach, heating thoroughly. In a large bowl, add spinach, onion mixture, egg substitute, and cheese. Mix well. Pour into a greased 9-inch pie plate. Bake for 35-45 minutes, or until quiche is golden brown. Slice into wedges and serve.
Makes 8 servings. 96 calories, 18.1 g fat, 458 mg sodium.

Zucchini Quiche

• JOCELYN M. PETERSON

Pastry:

1 cup whole wheat flour
1 cup bread flour
⅓ cup olive oil

Filling:

1 red onion, thinly sliced
1 tablespoon olive oil
1 large zucchini, sliced
6 ounces soy cheese, grated
2 tablespoons fresh basil, chopped
¼ cup egg substitute
1¼ cups soy milk
1 tablespoon McKay's Chicken Style Seasoning

Preheat oven to 400° F. Mix the flours together and add the olive oil and cold water to form a dough. Roll out the pastry and use it to line a 9- to 10-inch pie pan, ideally at least 1 inch deep. Prick the base of the pie shell with a fork, chill for 30 minutes, then cover with waxed paper or foil. Set pie pan on a baking sheet and bake for 20 minutes. Meanwhile, sauté the onion in the oil for 3 minutes until it is soft. Add the zucchini and fry for another 3 minutes. Spoon the onions and zucchini into the pastry shell. Scatter over most of the cheese and all the basil. Beat together the egg substitute, milk, and seasonings and pour over the filling. Top with the remaining cheese. Turn temperature down to 350° F and return the quiche to the oven for about 40 minutes, until it has risen and is just firm to the touch in the center. Allow to cool slightly before serving.
Makes 6 servings. 275 calories, 4 g fat, 60 mg sodium.

Tofu Surprise
• JOCELYN PETERSON

  1 pound frozen hard tofu (thawed, squeezed dry, and torn into bite-sized pieces)
  ¼ cup water
  2 tablespoons soy sauce (low-sodium)
  1 tablespoon peanut butter
  2 teaspoons onion powder
1½ teaspoons cumin
  ¼ teaspoon garlic powder
  2 tablespoons olive oil
  1 large green pepper, diced
  1 onion
  2 cloves garlic, minced
2½ cups cooked pinto beans
  1 tablespoon chili
  2 teaspoons Vege-Sal

Preheat oven to 350° F. Whip together water, soy sauce, peanut butter, onion powder, ½ teaspoon cumin, and garlic powder. Pour this over the prepared tofu pieces and squeeze in so that all liquid is absorbed evenly. Spread 1 tablespoon of olive oil on cookie sheet. Spread the tofu pieces on the oiled cookie sheet and bake 20 minutes. Flip them over and bake 10 minutes on the other side. Sauté green pepper, onion, and garlic in 1 tablespoon of olive oil in a heavy soup pot until tender. Add beans, water, chili powder, 1 teaspoon of cumin, Vege-Sal, and the baked tofu pieces to the pot. Bring to a simmer and serve hot.
Makes 10 servings. 300 calories, 5 g fat, 14 g protein, 250 mg sodium.

Chili Con Tofu With Beans
• JOCELYN PETERSON

  1 pound frozen hard tofu (thawed, squeezed dry, and torn into bite-sized pieces)
  ¼ cup water
  2 tablespoons soy sauce (low sodium)
  1 tablespoon peanut butter
  1 teaspoon onion powder

1½ teaspoons cumin (divided)
  ¼ teaspoon garlic powder
  2 tablespoons olive oil
  1 large green pepper, diced
  1 large onion, diced
  2 cloves garlic, minced
2½ cups cooked pinto beans
  1 tablespoon chili powder
  1 teaspoon Vege-Sal®

Preheat oven to 350° F. Whip together water, soy sauce, peanut butter, onion powder, ½ teaspoon cumin, and garlic powder. Pour this over the prepared tofu pieces and squeeze in so that all liquid is absorbed evenly. Spread 1 tablespoon olive oil on cookie sheet. Spread the tofu pieces on the oiled cookie sheet and bake 20 minutes. Flip them over and bake 10 minutes on the other side. Sauté green pepper, onion, and garlic in 1 tablespoon of olive oil in a heavy soup pot until tender. Add beans, water, chili powder, 1 teaspoon of cumin, Vege-Sal®, and the baked tofu pieces to the pot. Bring to a simmer and serve hot.
Makes 10 servings. 300 calories, 5 g fat, 14 g protein, 25 g carbohydrate, 250 mg sodium.

Tofu Fried Rice (Oriental)
• PAMELA WILLIAMS

  1 tablespoon soy oil
  3 cloves garlic, chopped
  1 onion, chopped
  2 tablespoons celery, chopped
  ½ cup steamed carrots, cut into thin strips
  ½ cup frozen peas, thawed
  4 cups cooked brown rice
  2 tablespoons low-sodium soy sauce
  1 cup broiled tofu (recipe below)
  1 green onion, chopped

Heat oil in saucepan and sauté garlic and onion until tender. Add celery, carrots, and peas and sauté for 2 minutes. Add rice and soy sauce and cook for another 2 minutes, stirring often. Add tofu and cook

2 minutes more. Sprinkle with green onion and cover for 3 minutes. Serve.
Makes 6 servings. 243 calories, 7 g fat, 776 mg sodium.

Broiled Tofu
• PAMELA WILLIAMS
- 8 ounces extra-firm tofu
- 1½ teaspoon vegetable oil
- 2 tablespoons low-sodium soy sauce
- ½ teaspoon sesame seed oil
- Dash of cayenne pepper

Place the tofu between two plates and gently press the tofu for about 2 minutes to remove water. Wrap tofu in a paper towel and gently squeeze out remaining water. Slice and place on a flameproof pan. In a small bowl mix vegetable oil, soy sauce, sesame seed oil, and a dash of cayenne pepper. Spoon some of this mixture over each piece of tofu. Broil on each side for 5 minutes or until brown and crisp. Serve as a side dish or in a sandwich.
Makes 4 servings. 60 calories, 4 g fat, 603 mg sodium.

Tofu Fried Rice (Oriental)
• RUTH DAVIS
- 2 cups brown rice (instant brown rice may be used)
- ½ pound diced tofu
- ½ bell pepper, finely chopped
- 1 cup onions, finely chopped
- ½ cup sliced almonds
- ½ teaspoon McKay's Chicken Style Seasoning
- ½ teaspoon oregano
- ¼ cup vegetable oil

Prepare brown rice as indicated on package. While rice is cooking, sauté tofu, bell pepper, onion, almonds, chicken-style seasoning, and oregano in vegetable oil over medium heat for 2½ minutes,

stirring constantly. When rice is cooked, add it to the sautéed ingredients and stir-fry 3-4 minutes.
Makes 4 servings. 334 calories, 21 g fat, 71 mg sodium.
COOK'S HINT: Vegetarian chicken-style meat may be substituted for diced tofu; however, the calories, fat, and sodium will be increased.

Tofu Meatballs
• PAMELA WILLIAMS
- 1 pound firm tofu, drained and mashed
- ½ cup mushrooms, finely chopped
- ½ cup potatoes grated
- 3 eggs (or egg substitute equivalent), beaten
- ½ cup breadcrumbs
- ¼ cup onions, minced
- 2 cloves garlic, minced
- ½ teaspoon thyme
- 1 tablespoon parsley
- ¼ teaspoon nutmeg
- Dash of cayenne pepper
Gravy
- 1 10-ounce can low-fat mushroom soup
- ½ can water

Meatballs: Preheat oven to 350° F. In a large bowl, mix all ingredients well. Spray cookie sheet with vegetable cooking spray. Roll mixture into 1½ inch balls and place on cookie sheet. Bake 10 minutes. Serve in mushroom gravy. Gravy: Mix soup and water. Heat for 5 minutes on low heat.
Makes 6 servings. 197 calories, 8.5 g fat, 871 mg sodium.

Tofu Steaks
• BARBARA FRAZIER

   1 block extra-firm tofu
  ¼ cup water
   4 teaspoons Braggs Liquid Aminos
   2 cloves garlic, thinly sliced
   1 tablespoon grated fresh ginger
   1 tablespoon extra-virgin olive oil

Remove tofu from package; rinse. Place tofu on its side on cutting board, thickly lined with paper towels. Cut tofu into ¼ inch portions to yield four steaks. Place steaks side by side on paper towels and cover steaks with thick pads of paper towels. With hands palm-down on steaks, press tofu to remove water. Repeat process as needed until tofu is dry. Pierce each tofu steak with forks in three places. Put cast iron skillet on stove and add olive oil. When oil is hot, remove steaks from paper towels and brown on both sides in skillet. Bring remaining ingredients to slow simmer in saucepan. Pour over browned tofu steaks.
Makes 5 servings. 46 calories, 4 g fat, 2 g protein, 178 mg sodium.
SERVING SUGGESTION: Serve with red/green peppers, brown rice, and steamed broccoli.

Roupa Velha (Brazil)
• PAMELA WILLIAMS

   1 small onion stuck with a clove
   2 carrots, peeled and cut in two
   1 celery stalk, cut in two
4-5 sprigs fresh parsley
   1 bay leaf
   2 cloves of garlic
  ½ teaspoon salt

Topping:

   1 tablespoon olive oil
   1 large onion, thinly sliced
   2 small tomatoes, blanched, peeled, and sliced
  ½ cup parsley, chopped
  ¼ teaspoon raw sugar

  ¼ teaspoon salt
    Cayenne pepper
16 ounces extra-firm tofu cut into thin strips
   2 tablespoons lemon juice
   2 tablespoons water

Soup: Add all ingredients to a stockpot. Add 4 cups of water and bring to a boil. Simmer for 1 hour. Remove vegetables and drain. Set aside. *Topping:* Heat oil in a frying pan and sauté onions until translucent. Add tomatoes, parsley, sugar, salt, and cayenne pepper to taste. Cook for another three minutes and add tofu mixture, lemon juice, and water. Stir and cook for another three minutes. Place tofu mixture in center of a larger serving plate. Surround with cooked brown rice or couscous.
Makes 4 servings. 180 calories, 1 g fat, 494 mg sodium.

Barbecued Tofu

   3 tablespoons peanut butter
  ⅓ cup oil
   1 tablespoon paprika
  ½ teaspoon garlic powder
  ¼ teaspoon cayenne pepper
   2 teaspoons salt
   2 pounds firm tofu, cut into strips, frozen, then thawed

Whip all ingredients except tofu until smooth. Pour over tofu strips and marinate 1 hour. Meanwhile, prepare barbecue sauce (see recipe below). When sauce is done, place tofu on cookie sheet coated lightly with oil. Bake at 350° F for about 25 minutes. Turn pieces and bake another 25 minutes until brown. Cover with barbecue sauce and bake 15 minutes more.

Barbecue Sauce
• PAT HUMPHREY

   1 medium onion, chopped
   2 cloves garlic, minced
  ⅓ cup oil
 2½ cups tomato sauce
  ¼ cup water
   1 cup brown sugar
   1 tablespoon molasses
 1½ teaspoons salt
  ¾ teaspoon cayenne
 1½ teaspoons dried parsley or
   1 tablespoon fresh parsley
  ½ cup lemon juice
   2 tablespoons soy sauce

Sauté onion and garlic in oil until onions are transparent. Add remaining ingredients except for lemon juice and soy sauce. Bring to a boil, reduce heat, and simmer for 1 hour. Add last two ingredients and simmer 10-15 minutes more.
Makes 12 servings (tofu with sauce). 276 calories, 19.7 g fat, 831 mg sodium.

Couscous With Vegetables (North Africa)
• PAMELA WILLIAMS

 1½ pound tofu, cut into cubes
   1 onion, chopped
   1 cup carrots, grated
   1 cup celery, cut into slices
   1 cup mushrooms, sliced
  ½ cup walnuts, chopped
   1 can chickpeas, drained
   1 8-ounce can tomato sauce
   2 tablespoons fresh parsley, chopped
 1½ cups water
  ½ teaspoon ginger
  ¼ teaspoon turmeric
   1 teaspoon cumin
  ¼ teaspoon garlic
   1 teaspoon paprika
  ½ teaspoon salt
   1 cup dry couscous

In large pan place brown tofu, onion, carrots, celery, mushrooms, and nuts. Add remaining ingredients except couscous and bring to boil. Cover and simmer for 40 minutes. Couscous: boil 1½ cups water with two tablespoons oil. Add couscous, stir, cover, reduce heat, and simmer for 5 minutes. Serve vegetables over steaming couscous.
Makes 4 servings. 566 calories, 17 g fat, 726 mg sodium.

Mock Turkey Loaf
• PAMELA AND ERMA WILLIAMS

   4 cups coarsely ground barley
   2 eggs (or egg substitute equivalent), beaten
  ⅔ cup milk
  ⅓ cup water
 1½ cups soft bread crumbs
  ½ cup celery
  ⅓ cup onion
    Dash of nutmeg
    Dash of dried rosemary
DRESSING:
  ½ cup brown rice
   1 cup water
   1 teaspoon McKay's Chicken Style Seasoning
   1 can mushroom soup
   1 cup nonfat sour cream
  ¼ cup chopped onion
   2 tablespoons oil
   1 egg (or egg substitute equivalent), beaten
  ½ teaspoon sage
   1 teaspoon paprika

Mix the first list of ingredients. Put half the mixture into 8" x 8" x 2" pan. Mix dressing ingredients and place on top of first mixture. Put the rest of the first mixture on top of the dressing ingredients. Bake at 350°F for 45 minutes. Cut into squares and serve with a mushroom or chicken flavored sauce.
Makes 12 servings. 238 calories, 6.4 g fat.

BEANS AND LEGUMES

For more recipes using beans and legumes, see Italian Cuisine on p. 95 and Mexican Cuisine on p. 98.

Bean Sausage
• DONNA GREEN GOODMAN

  2 cups pinto beans, cooked and drained
  1½ cups bread crumbs, plain
  4 tablespoons egg replacer
  ½ cup soy milk
  1 teaspoon salt (optional)
  ¾ teaspoon garlic powder
  1½ teaspoons sage
  ½ small onion, chopped fine
  ½ teaspoon Braggs Liquid Aminos

Mash beans. Mix with egg replacer and bread crumbs. Add remaining ingredients and mix well. Shape mixture into patties. Place on cookie sheet that has been sprayed with nonstick spray. Bake at 400°F until done. Serve as is, or cover with homemade gravy and let simmer about 20 minutes.
Makes 8 servings. 142 calories, 11 g fat, 141 mg sodium.

Bean Patties
• DONNA A. SMITH

  3½ cups cooked dry pinto beans
  2 cloves garlic
  ¾ cup Barbecue Sauce (recipe below)
  1 teaspoon cayenne pepper
  2 cups soft bread crumbs
  1 cup almond/rice shredded cheddar cheese
    Egg substitute, equivalent to 2 eggs
  ¼-⅓ cup oil
  ½ cup chunky salsa

Cook pinto beans according to directions on package. In food processor bowl add garlic and process until minced. Add beans, ¼ cup barbecue sauce, and pepper; process until mixture is smooth. Stir in 1 cup bread crumbs and cheese. Form mixture into patties. Brush both sides of patties with egg and coat with remaining bread crumbs. Refrigerate until ready to cook. Add oil and cook in pan until patties are browned on both sides. Combine remaining barbecue sauce and salsa.
Makes 4 servings. 129 calories, 4 g fat, 11 mg sodium.

Barbecue Sauce
• DONNA A. SMITH

  1 medium onion, minced
  2 garlic cloves, minced
  ⅓ cup oil
  2 8-ounce cans low-sodium tomato sauce
  ¼ cup water
  1 cup brown sugar
  1 tablespoon molasses
  1 teaspoon salt
  ¾ teaspoon cayenne pepper
  ½ cup lemon juice
  1 tablespoon soy sauce

Sauté onion and garlic in oil. Add remaining ingredients except for lemon juice and soy sauce. Bring mixture to boil, reduce heat, and simmer for 30 minutes. Add lemon juice and soy sauce.
Makes 2 cups (¼ cup per serving). 207 calories, 9 g fat, 394 mg sodium.

Old-fashioned Red Beans
• PAMELA AND ERMA WILLIAMS

  1 pound dry beans
  2 quarts water
  2 medium onions, chopped
  3 bay leaves
  1 large green bell pepper, chopped
  4 tablespoons chopped parsley
  4 cloves garlic, minced
  1½ teaspoons dried thyme
    Salt to taste

Remove bad beans, rinse, and drain remaining beans. In a large pot combine beans, water, onions, and bay leaves. Bring to a boil, reduce heat, cover, and cook for 1½ hours. Stir and mash beans against the pot. Add green pepper, parsley, garlic, thyme, and salt. Cook uncovered for 30 minutes. Remove bay leaves and serve over brown rice.

Makes 8 servings. 215 calories, 0 g fat.

Zippy Chili
• BARBARA FRAZIER

   2 15-ounce cans dark-red kidney beans
   1 package frozen stir-fry peppers/onions
   1 28-ounce can crushed tomatoes
   2 teaspoons each cumin and chili powder
      Dash of cayenne pepper or to taste

Drain beans and rinse with water. Combine all ingredients in large pot with ½ cup water. Stir, cover, and simmer for five to eight minutes.

Makes 4 servings. 46 calories, 7 g fat, 2.6 g protein, 152 mg sodium.

Garbanzos and Vegetables
• PAT HUMPHREY

   1 tablespoon olive oil
   1 medium onion, finely chopped
   2 cloves garlic, finely chopped
   2 cups carrots, sliced
   1 teaspoon ground coriander
   1 teaspoon chicken seasoning
   ½ teaspoon salt
   ¼ teaspoon ground turmeric
   ⅛ teaspoon cayenne
   2 medium zucchinis, sliced
   1 can garbanzos (chickpeas) with liquid

Sauté onion and garlic in oil over medium-high heat for 3 minutes. Add remaining ingredients; stir. Bring to a boil, then cover and reduce heat. Simmer about 15 minutes. Serve over couscous or rice.

Makes 8 servings. 62 calories, 2 g fat, 67 mg sodium.

Vegetarian Curry (India)
• JOHNETTA FRAZIER

   1 teaspoon soy margarine
   1 onion, sliced
   2 garlic cloves, minced
   1 apple, peeled and cored
  1½ teaspoons grated lemon peel
   1 teaspoon coriander
  1½ teaspoons curry
   1 teaspoon ginger
   ⅛ teaspoon turmeric
   1 16-ounce can kidney beans, undrained
   1 16-ounce can black eyed peas, drained
   ⅓ cup raisins
   ¼ cup soy yogurt
   3 cups brown rice
   ½ cup cilantro, chopped
   3 scallions, chopped
   ¼ cup peanuts, chopped

Sauté margarine, onion, garlic, and apple. Mix spices together and add to apple mixture. Add beans, peas, and raisins. Cover pan and allow to cook for 5 minutes. Remove from heat and stir in yogurt. Place 3 cups of hot brown rice in platter and cover with curried vegetables. Garnish top of vegetables with cilantro, scallions, and peanuts.

Makes 6 servings. 395 calories, 8 g fat, 319 mg sodium.

Beans and Ratatouille (Caribbean)
• JOHNETTA FRAZIER

   1 eggplant, cubed
   1 onion, chopped
   3 garlic cloves, minced
   7 large tomatoes
   1 cup cooked black-eyed peas
   1 chili pepper

Cook eggplant, onion, and garlic in a pan sprayed with Pam. Add remaining ingredients and season to taste.

Makes 6 servings. 179 calories, 1 g fat, 21 mg sodium.

Kidney Bean Delight

• JOCELYN M. PETERSON

    1 medium onion, chopped
    ½ cup green pepper, chopped
    1 tablespoon olive oil
    3 cups cooked kidney beans
    1 4-ounce can tomato sauce
    1 cup ground corn chips

Sauté onion and green pepper in oil. Mix with beans and tomato sauce in a casserole dish. Sprinkle top with corn chips. Bake at 350° F for 20 minutes. Serve with brown rice.

Makes 8 servings. 112 calories, 4 g protein, 1 g fat, 50 mg sodium.

Black Bean Cakes

• PAMELA WILLIAMS

    1 can black beans, undrained
    1 cup bread crumbs
    ½ cup tomato sauce
    ¼ cup onion, chopped
    1 egg (or egg substitute equivalent), beaten
    ¼ teaspoon salt
    2 strips of Morningstar Farms® Breakfast Strips®

Place undrained beans in a bowl and mash slightly. Add bread crumbs, tomato sauce, onion, egg, and salt. Break up two breakfast strips into small bits and add to mixture. Blend well. Turn into muffin tins and bake at 375° F for 35 minutes or until done. Remove cakes, cover with tomato sauce and garnish with strips.

Makes 4 servings. 235 calories, 9 g fat, 429 mg sodium.

Quick Vegetarian Black Bean Chili

• CHRISTINA FLEMING GABRIEL

    2 tablespoons vegetable oil
    1 large onion, chopped
  1⅔ cups vegeburger
    ½ teaspoon each: garlic powder, basil, oregano, and crushed red pepper
  1½ cups plain spaghetti sauce
    1 15½-ounce can black beans
    1 15½-ounce can red kidney beans

In a large pot over medium heat, add vegetable oil and onion. Sauté onion. Brown burger, then add garlic powder, basil, oregano, crushed red pepper, spaghetti sauce, and beans. Mix completely. Simmer for 15-20 minutes until chili is heated.

Makes 8 servings. 198 calories, 3.26 g fat, 1,004 mg sodium.

Black Beans, Caribbean Style

• PAMELA AND ERMA WILLIAMS

      Vegetable oil spray
  1½ cups chopped onion
    ½ cup chopped bell pepper
    3 garlic cloves, minced
    1 tablespoon ginger root, freshly grated
    1 teaspoon fresh thyme, chopped
    ½ teaspoon ground allspice
  4½ cups cooked black beans, drained
    ¾ cup water
    ¼ teaspoon salt
    3 tablespoons lemon juice

Spray pan with vegetable oil spray and saute onion, green pepper, and garlic until onions are translucent. Add ginger, thyme, and allspice and sauté for 2 minutes, stirring to keep from sticking. Stir in the beans, water, salt, and lemon juice. Cook on very low heat for about 15 minutes, stirring occasionally. Mixture will thicken slightly. Serve with rice.

Makes 4 servings. 273 calories, 1 g fat, 273 mg sodium.

Chickpea Loaf
• PAT HUMPHREY

     2 15-ounce cans chickpeas
     1 15-ounce can tomatoes
     1 small onion, chopped
     1 small clove garlic
     1 tablespoon canola oil
     1 teaspoon lemon juice
    1½ teaspoons salt
     1 teaspoon McKay's Chicken Style Seasoning
     ¼ cup fresh parsley, chopped
     ½ cup slivered almonds
    1½ cups cooked brown rice

Drain chickpeas, then blend in blender along with next eight ingredients. Pour into sprayed casserole dish, add almonds and rice. Bake at 375° F for 1 hour.
Makes 10 servings. 372 calories, 10.5 g fat, 349 mg sodium.

Garden Fresh Burgers
• PAMELA AND ERMA WILLIAMS

     2 10½-ounce cans chickpeas, drained
     1 cup finely chopped pecans
    1½ cups plain bread crumbs
    1¼ cups chopped spinach
     1 cup grated carrots
     ¼ cup chopped green bell pepper
     ¾ cup green onions, chopped
     1 tablespoon chopped celery
     1 tablespoon chopped parsley
     ¼ cup fat-free mayonnaise
        Nonstick cooking spray

Put chickpeas in food processor and chop. Combine chickpeas, pecans, bread crumbs, spinach, carrots, green bell peppers, onions, and celery, parsley, and mayonnaise. Shape into six patties. Brown patties on both sides in skillet sprayed with nonstick spray on low heat. Serve.
Makes 6 servings. 379 calories, 13 g fat.

Quick Lentil Patties
• PAT HUMPHREY

     1 small onion, chopped
     2 tablespoons oil
     2 cups cooked, mashed lentils
     ½ cup walnuts, chopped
     1 teaspoon Vege-Sal
     ¼ teaspoon garlic powder

Mix all ingredients and form into patties. Brown lightly on both sides in skillet sprayed with Pam. May also be baked at 375° F for 20 minutes, turning once.
Makes 8 servings. 124 calories, 8 g fat, 277 mg sodium.

Lentil Patties
• PAT HUMPHREY

     ½ cup dry lentils
     2 cups water
     1 teaspoon McKay's Chicken Style Seasoning
     1 large onion, chopped
     1 small green pepper, chopped
     1 tablespoon oil
     ½ teaspoon garlic powder
     ½ teaspoon sage
     ¼ teaspoon thyme
     1 cup herb-seasoned stuffing mix

Cook lentils in water until done. Drain lentils, saving liquid, and set aside. Saute onion, green pepper, and seasonings in oil; add to lentils. Add stuffing mix and enough reserved liquid to make mixture into patty consistency. Shape into patties and brown on both sides in medium-hot nonstick skillet sprayed with vegetable coating.
Makes 8 servings. 107 calories, 2.3 g fat, 278 mg sodium.

Rice and Beans (Caribbean)

- PAT HUMPHREY

    Vegetable oil spray
2 cloves garlic, chopped
1 tablespoon thyme
1 5-ounce can red beans
1¼ cups long-grain rice, uncooked
½ cup unsweetened coconut milk
1¾ cups water
1 medium onion, chopped
½ teaspoon salt

Spray vegetable oil spray in frying pan and sauté onions and garlic until brown. Drain beans and place in pot with all other ingredients. Cover and cook over a low heat for 20 to 30 minutes until all the liquid is absorbed by the rice.
Makes 6 servings. 237 calories, 5g fat, 332 mg sodium.

NUTS AND GRAINS

Irish Stew (Ireland)

- JUANITA ALEXANDER

2 cups Vegetable Stock (p. 38)
1 tablespoon Braggs Liquid Aminos
5 medium potatoes, diced
4 carrots, diced
2 medium turnip roots, diced
1 cup fresh or frozen lima beans
3 stalks of celery, sliced
1 cup fresh or frozen peas
2 medium onions, chopped
1 head cauliflower cut into florets
½ cup rinsed raw cashews
2 garlic cloves
½ medium onion
½ cup water
2 cups vegetable stock or water
½ teaspoon sea salt
1 teaspoon chicken-style seasoning
1 tablespoon Kitchen Bouquet
1 pie crust (optional)

In a soup pot, cook the first seven ingredients until tender. Arrange all vegetables in a deep roasting pan, adding the peas, onions and cauliflower. Blend the cashews, garlic, and onions in ½ cup water until smooth. Add the next four ingredients, blending well. Pour the gravy over the vegetables. Cover with the pie crust, and seal tightly around the edges. Bake in the oven at 350° F for approximately 1 hour or until the crust is nicely browned.
Makes 12 servings. 260 calories, 9 g fat, 170 mg sodium.

Macaroni and Cheez

- DONNA GREEN GOODMAN

2 quarts water
2 cups soy or whole wheat macaroni
1 cup cashews, clean and raw

2 cups water
1 four-ounce jar pimientos
2 tablespoons fresh lemon juice
2 teaspoons salt
1 teaspoon onion powder
¼ teaspoon garlic powder
Grated soy cheese or bread
Crumbs as topping (optional)

Bring 2 quarts water to boil, then add macaroni. Bring to second boil, reduce heat, and simmer covered until tender. While macaroni is cooking, blend cashews with 2 cups water until very smooth. Add remaining ingredients, except topping, and continue blending until smooth. Drain macaroni and add to sauce. Stir and place in a casserole dish (will be very watery). Cover and bake at 350° F for 30 minutes. Uncover and top with topping (optional). Bake another 5 to 10 minutes.
Makes 8 servings. 127 calories, 8 g fat, 363 mg sodium.
COOK'S HINT: For additional flavor add garlic powder, McKay's Chicken Style Seasoning, paprika, turmeric, and nutritional yeast flakes until desired taste is achieved.

Old-fashioned Sausage
• PAMELA AND ERMA WILLIAMS
2 cups water
½ teaspoon salt
½ cup hulled millet
½ teaspoon sage
1 cup finely chopped mushrooms
1 tablespoon butter
½ cup chopped walnuts
1 teaspoon minced onion
1 clove garlic, minced

Bring water to boil in heavy saucepan. Slowly stir in salt, millet, and sage. Bring to a boil, stirring constantly. Cover and turn heat low. Cook until water is absorbed. Saute mushrooms in 1 tablespoon of butter until brown. Stir mushrooms, walnuts, onion, and garlic into hot millet. Pack into a greased 8½-inch loaf pan. Chill several hours or overnight. Cut into slices. Dip into whole wheat flour and brown in nonstick skillet sprayed with Pam, browning both sides. Serve with mushroom sauce.
Makes 4 servings. 142 calories, 10 g fat.

Meatballs
• PAT HUMPHREY
½ cup walnuts
3 cups quick oats
1 onion
1 teaspoon salt
1 tablespoon soy sauce
¼ teaspoon sage
¼ teaspoon thyme
¼z teaspoon marjoram
2 cups nut milk (recipe below)
½ teaspoon garlic powder
½ teaspoon onion powder

Steam chopped onion in small amount of water. Mix steamed onion and remaining ingredients together. Let stand 15 minutes. Roll into small balls. Brown in pan (lightly coated with vegetable spray) or on a cookie sheet in oven.
Makes 8 servings. 237 calories, 11 g fat, 336 mg sodium.

Nut Milk (for savory recipes)
• PAT HUMPHREY
1 cup pecans or walnuts
1 cup hot water
¼ teaspoon salt
3 cups cold water

Blend nuts and hot water in blender. Add salt and remaining cold water. Blend thoroughly.

Walnut Roast

• RUTH DAVIS

- 1 cup soy milk
- 1 cup bread crumbs
- 1 cup ground walnuts
- 2 tablespoons chopped parsley
- 1 teaspoon garlic powder
- 1 teaspoon sage

Mix all ingredients together. Cover and let stand ½ hour. Place in oiled baking dish. Bake for one hour at 350° F. Serve with mushroom gravy and grits.
Makes 5 servings. 202 calories, 5.0 fat, 1 mg sodium.

Walnut Stuffing Balls

• JOCELYN PETERSON

- 4 cups bread crumbs
- 1 cup chopped walnuts
- ½ teaspoon thyme
- ½ teaspoon basil
- ½ cup chopped parsley
- ½ cup diced celery
- 1 onion, chopped
- ½ cup olive oil
- 2 vegetable bouillon cubes
- 1 cup boiling water

Sauté celery and onion in 1 tablespoon oil. Place bouillon cubes in water and set aside. Mix dry ingredients together, then add sautéed celery and onion, and the olive oil. Add just enough of the bouillon to moisten the mixture. Shape into 2-inch balls. Place on oiled baking sheet. Bake at 375° F for 20 minutes or until crisp.
Makes 3 servings. 200 calories, 2 g fat, 6 g protein.

Oat Pecan Burgers

• PAT HUMPHREY

- 4 cups water
- ½ cup Braggs Liquid Aminos
- ⅓ cup canola oil
- 1 cup pecans, chopped

- ¼ cup nutritional yeast
- 2 teaspoons garlic powder
- 1 tablespoon dried basil
- 2 teaspoons onion powder
- 1 teaspoon Bakon yeast
- 1 teaspoon coriander, ground
- 1 teaspoon dried sage
- 4 cups rolled oats

Place all ingredients except rolled oats in large pan, stir well, and bring to slow boil over medium-low heat. Stir in rolled oats and immediately remove from heat. Cover and set aside to cool. Preheat oven to 350° F. Form oat mixture into 3-inch patties and place on oiled baking sheets. Bake for 15 minutes on each side. (To form patties, use 3¼-inch metal ring such as that used to make English muffins. Place rings on cookie sheet, fill rings half full with burger mix, flatten out, lift rings, and presto! Perfect patties!)
Makes 20 servings. 120 calories, 7 g fat, 414 mg sodium.

Pecan Patties

• RUTH DAVIS

- 1 cup pecan meal
- 1 cup bread crumbs
- 1 cup soy meal
- 1 teaspoon garlic powder
- 1 teaspoon ground sage
- 1 teaspoon finely chopped parsley
- ½ cup diced onions

Combine all ingredients. Shape into patties. Place patties on baking sheet or greased baking dish. Bake at 350° F for 35-40 minutes, until brown. Serve with mushroom gravy over rice or grits.
Makes 4 servings. 257 calories. 21.4 g fat, 114.6 mg sodium.

Pecan Roast

• PAT HUMPHREY

- 1 cup cooked brown rice
- 4 cups whole wheat bread crumbs

1 cup finely chopped pecans
1½ cups water
1 medium onion, coarsely chopped
⅔ cup whole wheat flour
1 teaspoon sweet basil
1½ teaspoons salt

Combine brown rice, bread crumbs, and pecans in a bowl and set aside. Whiz rest of ingredients in blender, pour this mix over brown rice mixture, and stir. Place the mix in an oiled loaf pan and bake at 350° F for 1 hour.
Makes 8 servings. 214 calories, 9 g fat, 500 mg sodium.

Pecan Roast (low salt)
• JOCELYN PETERSON

1 cup cooked brown rice
4 cups whole wheat bread crumbs
½ cup chopped pecans
1½ cups water
1 medium onion chopped
1 cup whole wheat flour
1 teaspoon sweet basil
1 teaspoon thyme
2 tablespoons vegetarian seasonings
1 teaspoon cumin
1 teaspoon parsley

Combine brown rice, bread crumbs, and pecans in a bowl and set aside. Blend remaining ingredients, pour into rice mixture and stir. Place in an oiled loaf pan and bake at 350° F for 45 minutes.
Makes 12 servings. 200 calories, 5 g fat, 90 mg sodium.

Pecan Roast or Patties
• PAT HUMPHREY

2 cups pecans, chopped
1 cup cooked potatoes, diced
1 cup celery, chopped
1 small onion, chopped
1 4-ounce can tomato sauce

1 cup bread crumbs
  Vegex or Sovex to taste
1 tablespoon soy sauce
1 teaspoon salt
¼ teaspoon sweet basil

Roast: Sauté pecans, potatoes, celery, and onion in a heavy pan in a small amount of water until tender. Add remaining ingredients and mix well. Turn mixture into casserole sprayed with vegetable coating and bake at 350° F for 40 minutes.
Patties: Mash potatoes thoroughly with fork and grind nuts in blender. Sauté celery and onion, then combine all ingredients and shape into patties. Brown on both sides in nonstick skillet or in oven on a sprayed cookie sheet.
Makes 8 servings. 239 calories, 17 g fat, 496 mg sodium.

John's Mock Meatloaf
• DONNA A. SMITH

1½ cups oats
1 cup pecan meal
½ cup chopped onions
½ cup chopped green pepper
½ cup wheat germ
½ cup cooked rice
5 tablespoons nutritional yeast
¾ cup firm tofu (blended smooth)
¼ cup spaghetti sauce
1 teaspoon basil
1 teaspoon rosemary
2 teaspoons garlic powder
2 tablespoons flour
¼ cup Bragg Liquid Aminos

Mix all ingredients together. Cover and let stand for 10 minutes. Shape in the form of a loaf and place in a large loaf pan or on a greased baking dish. Bake at 350° F for approximately 30 minutes. Then pour about half the meatloaf sauce over loaf and bake another 10 minutes.
MEATLOAF SAUCE

2 8-ounce cans low-sodium tomato sauce
15 ounces water

1 cup canned onion rings
2 tablespoons Bragg Liquid Aminos
4 tablespoons molasses
4 tablespoons honey
1 tablespoon lemon juice
1 tablespoon garlic powder
Pinch cayenne pepper

Put all ingredients in a saucepan and stir on medium heat until thickened. Makes 3½ cups of sauce. Makes 10 servings of meatloaf. 232 calories, 13 g fat, 409 mg sodium.

COOK'S HINT: The other half of the sauce recipe can be used for other meatless items, or more sauce can be used if desired.

Mock Meat Loaf

• PAMELA AND ERMA WILLIAMS

½ cup mushrooms, finely chopped
1 medium green bell pepper, finely chopped
1 medium onion, finely chopped
1 carrot, finely shredded
Olive oil for sautéing
2 cups fresh bread crumbs
2 cups pecans, finely chopped
1 medium tomato, chopped
1 egg (or egg substitute equivalent), lightly beaten
1 teaspoon dried basil
¾ teaspoon dried rosemary
Salt to taste

Preheat oven to 350° F. Oil an 8" x 4" loaf pan. Sauté mushrooms, bell pepper, onion, and carrots in olive oil until vegetables are soft. Add remaining ingredients to vegetables and mix well. Put mixture in the loaf pan and pack lightly. Bake for 40 minutes or until brown. Makes 6 servings. 289 calories, 15 g fat, 263 mg sodium.

Vegetarian Roast

• PAMELA AND ERMA WILLIAMS

1 cup cooked brown rice
4 eggs (or egg substitute equivalent), beaten
1½ tablespoons oil
1 teaspoon sage
½ teaspoon thyme
1 teaspoon Vegex
1 small onion, chopped
½ cup milk
1 cup cooked lentils
1 large potato, cooked and peeled
1 cup pecan pieces
½ cup bread crumbs
Salt

Blend rice with one beaten egg in an oiled skillet. Stir until light brown. Place in food processor and gradually add other ingredients except milk, seasonings, Vegex, and remaining eggs. Combine everything and mix well. Put in a double boiler and steam for 4 hours. Makes 10 servings. 150 calories, 6.2 g fat.

Almond Eggplant Patties

• JOCELYN PETERSON

2 regular-size eggplants
1 tablespoon McKay's Chicken Style Seasoning
1 tablespoon garlic powder
1 teaspoon olive oil
1 cup chopped almonds
½ cup breading meal or cornmeal
½ cup bread crumbs

Bake the eggplants until tender. When cooled, remove skin and mince the inside. Add the McKay's Chicken Style Seasoning, garlic powder, and oil. Then add almonds, breading meal, and bread crumbs. Form into patties. Bake or fry until brown. Makes 10 servings. 80 calories, 1 g fat, 30 mg sodium.

Orange Couscous (Morocco)
• PAMELA WILLIAMS

    1 cup almonds, chopped
    1 onion, chopped
    ½ green pepper, chopped
    2 cups orange juice
    2 cinnamon sticks
    5 cloves, whole
    ¼ teaspoon turmeric
    ¼ teaspoon ground red pepper
    ¼ teaspoon salt
    2 cups couscous
    ½ cup green onions, chopped

Spray a large saucepan with vegetable oil and cook almonds on a low heat until lightly toasted. Add onions and green pepper; cook for two minutes or until soft. Add orange juice, cinnamon sticks, cloves, turmeric, red pepper, and salt, and bring to a boil. Quickly stir in couscous, cover, and turn off heat. Let stand for 5 minutes or until liquid is absorbed. Sprinkle each portion with green onions.
Makes 6 servings. 240 calories, 12 g fat, 98 mg sodium.

MEAT SUBSTITUTES
Sautéed Burger Potatoes
• RUTH DAVIS

    6 potatoes, cleaned and thinly sliced
    2 tablespoons vegetable oil
    1 onion, finely chopped
    ½ cup bell pepper, finely chopped
    ½ can Loma Linda Redi-Burger, crumbled
    ½ teaspoon garlic powder
    ¼ teaspoon paprika

Stir-fry ingredients together in a large frying pan for 20-25 minutes over medium heat until potatoes are tender. Precooked potatoes will shorten cooking time. Stir often to prevent sticking. Garnish with parsley if desired.
Makes 6 servings. 257 calories, 6.2 g fat, 46.2 mg sodium.

Vege-Quick Loaf
• PAT HUMPHREY

    1 16-ounce can vegetarian burger
    ½ 8-ounce package herb seasoned stuffing
    1 large onion, finely chopped
    ½ bell pepper, chopped
    1 stick celery, chopped
    ½ teaspoon garlic powder
    ½ 32-ounce jar chunky-style spaghetti sauce
    2 teaspoons sage
    ⅛ teaspoon cayenne
    1 can Italian-style tomato paste
    1 heaping tablespoon honey
    2 tablespoons crushed pineapple
      Salt to taste

Mix well first 10 ingredients and place into a flat loaf pan. For glaze, mix tomato paste, honey, and pineapple. Bake loaf approximately 20 minutes at 350° F. Then top with glaze and bake 10 more minutes.
Makes 16 servings. 115 calories, 3.3 g fat, 312 mg sodium (without added salt).
COOK'S HINT: Save time by chopping the vegetables in a food processor.

Summer Squash Delight
• PAT HUMPHREY

    1 medium onion, sliced
    1 green pepper, cut in strips
    1 2-ounce can mild green chilies
    2 yellow squash, sliced
    1 package Worthington® Grillers®

Sauté onion and green pepper in skillet in small amount of water until tender. Add green chilies, ½ sliced yellow squash, 4 crumbled Grillers. Cook until squash is tender. Add salt to taste.
Makes 8 servings. 161 calories, 7 g fat, 264 mg sodium.

Stuffed Plantains

• PAMELA WILLIAMS

    4 ripe plantains, peeled
       Vegetable oil spray (butter-flavored)
    4 Worthington® Stripples® chopped
    1 teaspoon cornstarch
    ¼ cup plain bread crumbs
    1 tablespoon grated cheddar cheese

Preheat oven to 400° F. Halve plantains lengthwise. Scoop out pulp from the middle with a teaspoon. Set aside pulp. Spray shells with vegetable oil spray. In a medium bowl, mash pulp until smooth. Fold in Stripples®, cornstarch, bread crumbs, and cheese. Fill plantain shells with mixture. Bake 15 minutes and serve hot. Serve with rice and beans.
Makes 4 servings. 209 calories, 2 g fat, 142 mg sodium.

Quick Skillet Steak

• PAT HUMPHREY

    1 onion, chopped
    1 large green pepper, chopped
    3 stalks celery, chopped
    1 can Worthington® Prime Stakes
    1 can tomato soup
       Water

Sauté vegetables in skillet in small amount of water. Rinse gravy from Prime Steaks and place them in skillet with vegetables. Mix tomato soup and 1 can of water. Add to skillet and simmer over medium heat for 10-15 minutes.
Makes 4 servings. 140 calories, 7.2 g fat, 476 mg sodium.

Eggplant Deluxe

• PAT HUMPHREY

    1 large green onion, diced
    ¼ green pepper, diced
    2 large cloves garlic, minced
    3 tablespoons oil

    1 20-ounce can Loma Linda® Vege-Burger®
    1 teaspoon Vegex®
    1 teaspoon oregano
       Salt (optional)
    1 medium eggplant, peeled and sliced
    2 cups spaghetti sauce
    ½ cup Parmesan Cheeze (recipe below)

Sauté onion, garlic, and green pepper with oil for a couple of minutes. Add burger to vegetables and continue to sauté about 5 minutes. Add Vegex® oregano, and salt (optional) to this mixture. Place all ingredients in layers in coated shallow baking dish, starting with eggplant, and following with burger mixture, spaghetti sauce, and Parmesan cheese. Bake 1 hour at 375° F.
Makes 6 servings. 257 calories, 18.6 g fat, 351 mg sodium.

Parmesan Cheeze

• PAT HUMPHREY

    1 cup lightly toasted sesame seeds
    ¼ cup yeast flakes
    ½ teaspoon onion powder
    ¼ teaspoon garlic powder
    ½ teaspoon salt

Place all ingredients in a dry seed mill or blender. Mill until seeds are ground and ingredients are thoroughly combined.
96 calories, 8.5 g fat, 106 mg sodium.

Vegetarian Roast Turkey

• PAMELA AND ERMA WILLIAMS

    3½ cups cooked and drained lentils (save liquid)
    2 onions, chopped
    1 cup potatoes, boiled, peeled, and cut into chunks
    8 slices Worthington® mock turkey
    1 tablespoon ground sage
    2 tablespoons milk
    2 eggs (or egg substitute equivalent)

1½ cups walnuts
½ cup bread crumbs
⅓ cup milk
2 tablespoons oil
¼ cup lentil juice
Salt to taste

Grind first four ingredients. Place half the mixture in an oiled pan. Mix the rest of the ingredients to make the dressing. Place dressing on top of the first mixture in the pan. Place the rest of the first ingredients on top. Shape like a turkey roast. Brush with milk. Preheat oven to 400° F. Bake covered with aluminum foil tent for 30 minutes, then reduce heat to 300° F. Bake until done in the middle. Bake uncovered for the last 30 minutes.
Makes 14 servings. 175 calories, 6.7 g fat.

Stuffed Shells (Italy)
• PAT HUMPHREY
1 package large macaroni shells
1 recipe Ricotta-style Filling (recipe below)
1 recipe Italian Sauce (recipe below)

Cook macaroni shells according to package directions. Stuff shells with Ricotta-style Filling. Top with Italian Sauce and bake at 350° F for approximately 30 minutes or until hot and bubbly.
Makes 8 servings. 380 calories, 8 g fat, 720 mg sodium.
COOK'S HINT: If you're in a hurry, substitute store-bought spaghetti sauce for the Italian Sauce. Or make a large quantity of Italian Sauce ahead of time and freeze it for use when needed.

Ricotta-Style Filling (Italy)
• PAT HUMPHREY
2 16-oz. containers tofu firm
¼ cup fresh or frozen lemon juice
4 teaspoons honey
2 teaspoons salt
4 teaspoons basil leaves
1 teaspoon garlic powder

After thoroughly draining tofu, mash it with a potato masher. Mix remaining ingredients with tofu.
Makes 4 cups. 80 calories, 3 g fat, 553 mg sodium.

Italian Sauce
• PAT HUMPHREY
1½ cups onion, chopped
1 green pepper, chopped
2 tablespoons cold-pressed olive oil
3 tablespoons water
4 cloves garlic, minced
2 6-oz cans tomato paste
4 cups canned tomatoes
1 tablespoon honey
2 teaspoons sweet basil
½ teaspoon marjoram
½ teaspoon oregano
1¼ teaspoon salt

Sauté onions, green pepper, and garlic in olive oil and water. Add rest of ingredients. Simmer for 1 hour. Sauce can be used for lasagna, spaghetti, or pizza.
Makes 12 quarts. 170 calories, 4.5 g fat, 503 mg sodium.

Eggplant Lasagna (Italy)
• PAT HUMPHREY
1 medium eggplant, peeled and sliced
1 large onion, halved and sliced
1 tablespoon olive oil
1 cup tomato sauce
2 cups canned tomatoes, drained, cut up
2 teaspoons honey
1 teaspoon garlic salt
½ teaspoon sweet basil
¼ teaspoon oregano
½ cup raw wheat germ
½ cup flour
2 cups of Ricotta-style Filling (recipe above) or low-fat cottage cheese
⅔ cup pitted black olives, sliced

Main Dishes

Parboil eggplant in small amount of water 6 minutes; drain. Sauté onion in olive oil. Add tomato sauce, tomatoes, and seasonings. Simmer 5 minutes. Mix wheat germ and flour. Then layer tomato mixture, eggplant slices, Ricotta-style Filling (recipe above), olives, and wheat germ/flour mixture, in that order, in an oblong baking dish. Repeat, ending with tomato mixture. Bake at 350° F for 30 minutes.
Makes 10 servings. 145 calories, 4.8 g fat, 617 mg sodium.

Tofu and Pasta (Italy)
• PAMELA WILLIAMS

    4 cloves garlic, minced
    ½ cup red onions, minced
    2 pounds extra-firm tofu, cubed
    2 tablespoons water
   3½ tablespoons low-sodium soy sauce
    ½ cup lightly steamed broccoli florets, chopped
    2 tablespoons fresh basil, chopped
    2 tablespoons fresh parsley, chopped
    2 cups cooked pasta
       Olive oil spray

Spray small pan with olive oil spray. Sauté onion and garlic over medium heat until onions are tender. Add tofu and cook for 5 minutes, stirring occasionally. Add water, soy sauce, and broccoli and cook for 5 more minutes. Add basil and parsley, and toss with pasta. Serve immediately.
Makes 6 servings. 148 calories, 5 g fat, 106 mg sodium.

Pasta e Fagioli (Italy)
• PAT HUMPHREY

   1¼ cups dried navy beans
    ¼ cup olive oil
   1½ teaspoons salt
    1 bay leaf
    3 cloves garlic
    3 carrots, diced
    2 small stalks celery, chopped
    1 large onion, chopped
    3 tablespoons olive oil
    2 cloves garlic, crushed
    1 teaspoon dried oregano
    ½ teaspoon dried basil
    6 ripe tomatoes, peeled, quartered
    ½ pound shell macaroni
       Fresh parsley, chopped

Soak beans in 6 cups water overnight. In the morning, place beans and water in large kettle and add next four ingredients. Simmer beans 2 to 3

hours until tender. Drain, reserving liquid, and discarding garlic and bay leaf. Sauté carrots, celery, and onions in hot olive oil; add garlic and seasonings. Cook 30 minutes, then add half the tomatoes, cover and cook another 15 minutes. Cook macaroni until barely tender. Combine beans, vegetables, and pasta in large pot, add 1½ cups reserved liquid and remaining tomatoes. Cover and simmer another 15 minutes, stirring occasionally. Serve hot on large platter and garnish with parsley.
Makes 10 servings. 268 calories, 10 g fat, 354 mg sodium.

Italian Baked Beans (Italy)

• PAT HUMPHREY

- 1 pound dried kidney or lima beans
- 4 cups water
- 1 large onion, chopped
- 3 tablespoons olive oil
- 1 small eggplant, sliced, pared, cubed
- 1 16-oz. can tomatoes
- 2 teaspoons salt
- 1 teaspoon leaf marjoram, crushed
- ½ cup water

Rinse and sort beans, place in large pot, and add water. Bring to boil for 2 minutes, remove from heat, cover, and let stand 1 hour. Bring beans to boil, reduce heat, and simmer 1 hour. Meanwhile in large skillet, sauté onion in olive oil, and set it aside. In same pan, sauté eggplant until soft. Stir in tomatoes, salt, and marjoram; simmer 5 minutes. Drain beans, reserving liquid. Combine beans and eggplant mixture in an electric slow cooker. Stir in water and 1 cup of reserved bean liquid. Cover and cook on low for 10 hours, or on high for 6 hours, until beans are tender.
Makes 8 servings. 156 calories, 6 g fat, 971 mg sodium.

Italian Meatballs (Italy)

• PAT HUMPHREY

- 1 can vegeburger
- 8 ounces herb-seasoned stuffing
- ¼ cup onion, finely chopped
- 1 teaspoon Italian seasoning
- ½ teaspoon garlic powder
- ½ cup chunky-style spaghetti sauce or Italian Sauce (p. 95)

Combine all ingredients in bowl. Mix thoroughly and form into balls. Bake on a sprayed cookie sheet for 20 to 30 minutes at 350° F.
Makes 6 servings. 281 calories, 12 g fat, 758 mg sodium.

Spaghetti With Vegeburger Sauce (Italy)

• PAMELA AND ERMA WILLIAMS

-    Nonstick cooking spray
- 1 large yellow onion, chopped
- 2 cloves garlic, minced
- 1 large green bell pepper, chopped
- 1 28-ounce can chopped tomatoes
- 1 teaspoon dried oregano
- 1 tablespoon dried parsley
- ½ teaspoon dried thyme
- 1 can Vegeburger
- 1 pound spaghetti

Coat a large skillet with non-stick cooking spray and heat over low heat. Add onions, garlic, and bell pepper; stir for one minutes. Add tomatoes, spices, and burger. Cover and cook for 15 minutes, stirring occasionally. Uncover and cook for 125 minutes longer. Meanwhile, cook spaghetti according to package directions. Drain. Serve sauce over spaghetti.
Makes 6 servings. 490 calories, 10 g fat.

Stewed Cabbage With Spaghetti (Italy)

• CHRISTINA FLEMING-GABRIEL

     2 tablespoons vegetable oil
     1 medium head green cabbage, thinly sliced
     1 medium onion, chopped
     ½ teaspoon garlic powder
     ¼ teaspoon each of basil and oregano
     ½ cup sliced stewed tomatoes
     1 8-ounce box thin spaghetti, prepared according to package directions.

In a 1½–quart Dutch oven, heat vegetable oil over medium heat. Add cabbage, onions, and seasonings. Stir frequently. When cabbage is just about tender, add stewed tomatoes. Reduce heat and simmer until done. Prepare spaghetti according to package directions. Serve stewed cabbage over spaghetti. Makes 4 servings. 156 calories, 6.4 g fat, 74 mg sodium.

Italian Stuffed Peppers (Italy)

• PAT HUMPHREY

     4 large green peppers
     ¼ cup olive oil
     1 cup dried bread crumbs
     4 tablespoons raisins
    12 black olives, pitted and chopped
    2½ tablespoons parsley, chopped
     1 tablespoon chopped basil
     1 teaspoon salt

Wash and core peppers. Mix rest of ingredients together and stuff peppers. Place peppers into a deep baking dish and bake at 375° F for one hour. Makes 4 servings. 223 calories, 16 g fat, 1,015 mg sodium.
HEALTHY OPTION: Reduce or omit oil for low-fat diets.

Italian Tomato Pie (Italy)

• PAT HUMPHREY

     3 medium russet potatoes, peeled, sliced
     ¼ cup olive oil
     ½ teaspoon salt
     1 small onion, chopped
     2 cloves garlic, minced
     ½ green pepper, finely diced
     3 small tomatoes, diced
     1 cup Italian Sauce (p. 95)
       Egg substitute (equivalent of 3 eggs)
     1 cup frozen peas

Preheat oven to 375° F. Cook potatoes in 2½ tablespoons hot olive oil over medium-high heat, stirring often, for 8 to 10 minutes. Place potatoes in bottom of 10-inch pie plate, and add salt to taste. Sauté onion, garlic, and green pepper 2 to 3 minutes in 1½ tablespoons oil. Add diced tomatoes and cook about 3 minutes until mixture thickens slightly. Stir in Italian Sauce and remove from heat. Whisk beaten egg substitute into sauce. Stir in peas. Pour mixture into pie pan lined with potatoes. Bake 30 to 35 minutes until set. Let stand 10 minutes before cutting. Makes 6 servings. 234 calories, 11 g fat, 457 mg sodium.

Spinach and Carrot Fettuccine (Italy)

• PAT HUMPHREY

     1 12-ounce package fettuccine
     2 tablespoons low-fat margarine
     1 cup green pepper, finely chopped into matchstick strips
     ¾ cup onion, finely chopped
    1½ teaspoons lemon juice
     2 10-ounce packages frozen spinach, thawed
     1 cup shredded carrots
    1¼ teaspoons garlic salt
    1¼ teaspoons dill weed

Cook fettuccine according to package directions; drain. Melt margarine in medium-sized skillet over

medium heat. Add pepper and onion; cook 5 minutes more. Add remaining ingredients, stirring occasionally. Toss fettuccine with spinach mixture.
Makes 4 servings. 403 calories, 4.4 g fat, 480 mg sodium.

Basic Beans (Mexico)

• PAT HUMPHREY

- 1¼ cups pinto beans
- 1 large yellow onion, sliced
- 2 cloves garlic, crushed
- 4 cups water
- 1 teaspoon salt
  Fresh cilantro, chopped

Soak beans overnight in cold water. In the morning, drain beans and place in a saucepan with sliced onion, garlic, and water. Bring to a boil, cover, and simmer gently for 1½ hours or until beans are tender. After beans have cooked, add salt to taste (about 1 teaspoon) and continue to cook until liquid thickens. Serve with chopped cilantro.
Makes 4 servings. 212 calories, 1.5 g fat.

Refried Beans (Mexico)

- 1 onion, chopped
- 2 garlic cloves, crushed
- 2 tablespoons oil
  Double recipe Basic Beans (above)

Sauté onion and garlic in oil. Add beans, then add a little liquid and mash the beans. Add beans and/or liquid while simmering over low heat until mixture becomes thick. Serve hot or chilled.
Makes 8 servings. 256 calories, 5.3 g fat, 537 mg sodium.

Whole-Wheat Tortillas (Mexico)

- 2 tablespoons corn oil
- 1½ cups whole wheat flour
- 1 teaspoon salt
- ½ to ¾ cup cold water

Add oil to flour and salt, then add enough water to make a soft dough. Divide into 12 small balls and roll or press in tortilla press (available at Mexican stores) into 8-inch circles. Bake for 30 seconds on each side on a hot, ungreased griddle, turning tortillas to each side several times until lightly browned.
Makes 12 servings. 138 calories, 32 g fat, 334 mg sodium.

Corn Tortillas (Mexico)

• PAT HUMPHREY

- 1½ cups cornmeal
- 1½ cups whole wheat flour
- ¾ teaspoon salt
- 3 tablespoons oil
- ¾ cup warm water

Combine cornmeal, flour, and salt in bowl. Add oil, using a fork to blend. Add warm water and stir until mixture is moistened. (If dough is too stiff, add a teaspoon or more of water.) Turn onto a floured surface and knead five minutes or until mixture is no longer sticky. Shape into 14 balls. Roll each into a thin 6-inch circle. Bake on a hot ungreased griddle for 1 minute on each side.
Makes 14 servings. 85 calories, 2.4 g fat, 110 mg sodium.

Tamale Pie (Mexico)

• JOCELYN PETERSON

- 2 cups corn bread mix
- 1 cup water
- 2 cups cooked black-eyed peas
- ½ cup corn flakes
- ¼ cup tomato puree

1 teaspoon garlic powder
1 teaspoon cumin powder
2 tablespoons dried parsley
1 teaspoon McKay's Chicken Style Seasoning

Combine corn bread mix with water. Spread corn bread mix in a 9-inch pie pan. Mix all other ingredients together and pour over the corn bread mix. Bake at 350° F for 30-40 minutes.
Makes 8 servings. 250 calories, 2 g fat, 80 mg sodium.

Seven-Layer Burrito (Mexico)
• PAT HUMPHREY

1 cup brown rice
2½ cups water
1 medium onion, chopped
2 cans black beans
2 cloves garlic, minced
1 tablespoon cumin
2 medium bell peppers, chopped
4 medium tomatoes, chopped
1 cup salsa
1 medium avocado
1 teaspoon garlic powder
8 tortillas
1 package Sour Supreme (sour cream substitute)
1 package sliced soy cheese, mozzarella style

Cook rice according to package directions. Meanwhile, in large skillet sauté onion in water or oil until tender. Add 2 cans drained black beans, garlic, cumin, peppers, 2 cups tomatoes, and ½ cup of salsa. Cook over medium heat for about 10 minutes. Reduce heat and cook on low until rice is done. Add rice to bean mixture. Salt to taste. In small bowl, mash avocado, and season with garlic and salt to make guacamole. Place in center of tortillas: bean and rice mixture, grated tofu cheese, lettuce, tomatoes, 1 tablespoon Sour Supreme, 1 tablespoon guacamole, and 1 tablespoon salsa. Roll up tortillas and serve with additional salsa, if desired.
Makes 8 servings. 521 calories, 14 g fat, 497 mg sodium.

Tortilla Casserole (Mexico)

1 large onion, chopped
1 pound textured vegetable protein (TVP) granules (or frozen Crumbles or Vegeburger)
1 tablespoon olive oil
½ teaspoon No-alarm Chili Powder (recipe below)
2 8-ounce cans tomato sauce
2 cups canned, fresh, or frozen whole kernel corn
10-12 tortillas
1 cup Cashew Pimento Cheez (recipe below)

Sauté onion and TVP or burger in oil. Add chili powder, tomato sauce, and corn. Coat a 9" x 13" baking dish with nonstick cooking spray. Place five or six tortillas on bottom of pan; cover with half the filling. Layer remaining tortillas, tomato sauce, and cheese sauce. Bake at 350° F for 25 minutes.
Makes 6 servings. 410 calories. 11.5 g fat, 1,496 mg sodium.

No-Alarm Chili Powder
• PAT HUMPHREY

8 bay leaves
1½ teaspoons sweet basil leaves
¼ cup dried parsley flakes
1½ tablespoons onion powder
½ cup paprika
3 tablespoons cumin seed

Combine all ingredients and grind to a powder in blender. Store in an airtight container.

Cashew Pimento Cheez
• PAT HUMPHREY

- 1 cup raw cashews, rinsed
- ¼ cup pimento, diced
- 1 cup water
- 1 tablespoon onion powder
- 2 teaspoons lemon juice
- 1 tablespoon food yeast
- 1¼ teaspoons salt

Whiz cashews, pimento, and water in blender for 10 minutes. Add rest of ingredients and whiz briefly. Makes 2 cups. 84 calories, 7 g fat, 157 mg sodium.

Enchiladas (Mexico)
• PAT HUMPHREY

- 12 whole wheat Tortillas (p. 99)
- 1 cup Refried Beans (p. 99)
- 1 cup Cashew Pimento Cheez (recipe above)
- 1 large onion, chopped
- ½ cup olives, sliced
- 2 teaspoons No-alarm Chili Power (recipe above)
- ½ teaspoon cumin powder
  Enchilada Sauce (recipe below)
- 2 green onions, chopped
- 2 tomatoes, diced
- 1 avocado, sliced

Cover tortillas with plastic wrap and heat in microwave for 1 minute. Fill tortillas with Refried Beans, Cashew Pimento Cheez, onions, and olives. Sprinkle with No-alarm Chili Powder and cumin powder. Roll up tortillas and place seam side down in oblong baking disk. Cover with generous amount of Enchilada Sauce and bake at 350° F for 30 minutes. Top with onions, tomatoes, and avocado and serve.
Makes 6 servings. 584 calories, 24.6 g fat, 1,355 mg sodium.
COOK'S HINT: To reduce fat, omit avocado and/or Cashew Pimento Cheez.

Enchilada Sauce (Mexico)
• PAT HUMPHREY

- 1 can tomato paste
- 1 medium onion, chopped
- 2 cans tomato sauce
- 3 sauce cans water
- 1 teaspoon salt
- 1 teaspoon No-alarm Chili Powder (p. 100)
- 1 teaspoon ground cumin
- 1 teaspoon ground oregano
- 1 teaspoon garlic powder
- 1 teaspoon honey

Combine all ingredients in saucepan and bring to a boil. Reduce heat and simmer for 20 minutes.
Makes 3 cups. Per serving: 75 calories, 2.9 fat, 529 mg sodium.

Hot Taco Rice
• PAT HUMPHREY

- 1 onion, chopped
- 1 16-ounce can vegetarian burger
- 1½ cups medium salsa
- 1 teaspoon chicken seasoning
- 1 can tomato sauce
- 2 cups hot cooked brown rice
  Soy cheese, shredded (optional)
  Sour cream (optional)

Sauté onion in small amount of water, then add burger. Add salsa, chicken seasoning, and tomato sauce. Serve over hot cooked rice and garnish with chopped tomatoes, olives, shredded soy cheese (optional), and sour cream (optional).
Makes 6 servings: 281 calories, 8 g fat, 1,297 mg sodium.

Main Dishes

Veggie Fajitas (Mexico)
- PAT HUMPHREY

      1 tablespoon garlic powder
      1 tablespoon chili powder
      1 teaspoon paprika
      1 teaspoon dried basil
      1 package Worthington Grillers
     ½ cup green bell pepper, sliced
     ½ cup red bell pepper, sliced
      1 cup onion, sliced
      2 tablespoons oil
      8 flour tortillas
     ½ cup tomatoes, chopped
      2 cups lettuce, shredded
     ¼ cup avocado, peeled and chopped
     ¼ cup sour cream
      1 cup salsa

Mix garlic powder, chili powder, paprika, and basil in small bowl. Cut Grillers into strips and sprinkle with seasoning mix. Saute peppers and onion in oil until tender. Add Grillers and cook until heated. Place 4 tablespoons of Griller mixture in each tortilla. Add tomatoes, lettuce, avocado, and sour cream. Roll up tortilla and top with salsa.
Makes 8 servings. 200 calories, 9 g fat, 402 mg sodium.

Tamale Loaf
- PAT HUMPHREY

      2 cups cut corn
      3 cups canned tomatoes
      1 large onion, chopped
      1 6-ounce cans pitted olives, quartered
      2 teaspoons salt
      1 large clove garlic
     ⅓ cup unbleached white flour
      1 cup nut milk (p. 89)
      1 cup cornmeal
     ½ teaspoon cumin
     ½ teaspoon paprika

Boil the first 6 ingredients for 20 minutes. Mix remainder of ingredients. Add to tomato mixture. Bake in a 9" x 9" casserole dish for 1 hour at 325° F. Makes 8 servings. 167 calories, 5 g fat, 1,003 mg sodium.

Tostadas (Mexico)
- PAT HUMPHREY

         Refried Beans (p. 99)
     12 tostada shells
      ½ head lettuce, shredded
      2 large tomatoes, chopped
         Brandon's Guacamole (recipe below)

Spread Refried Beans on tostada shells, then top with shredded lettuce, tomatoes, and guacamole. Makes 6 servings. 600 calories, 22.6 g fat, 950 mg sodium.
COOK'S HINT: If possible, purchase tostada shells from a Mexican store—they taste great!

Brandon's Guacamole
- PAT HUMPHREY

      2 avocados
     ¼ teaspoon salt
      1 tablespoon crushed pineapple
      1 teaspoon garlic powder
         Dash cayenne

½ teaspoon McKay's Chicken Style Seasoning (optional)

Mash avocados with fork until mixture becomes a paste. Add remaining ingredients to taste.
Makes 8 servings. 108 calories, 11.3 g fat, 64 mg sodium.

Tasty Tostadas (Mexico)
• PAT HUMPHREY

- 1 recipe Bulgar Burger (recipe below)
- 1 medium onion, chopped
- 1 medium bell pepper, chopped
- 2 cloves garlic, minced
- 1 tablespoon water
- 1 8-ounce can tomato sauce
- 1 cup tomatoes, chopped
- 1 teaspoon paprika
- ½ teaspoon cumin
- 8 tostada shells
- 2 medium tomatoes, chopped
- 2 cups lettuce, shredded
- 1 cup soy cheese, American-style, shredded
- 1 cup salsa
- 1 package Tofutti Sour Supreme

To make taco filling, moisten Bulgur Burger with a small amount of water to soften. Simmer onion, bell pepper, and garlic in water until tender. Add Bulgur Burger and remaining ingredients. Heat thoroughly, stirring occasionally. Layer tortilla shells with taco filling, chopped tomatoes, shredded lettuce, shredded tofu cheese, and salsa. Top with dollop of Tofutti Sour Supreme.
Makes 8 servings. 177 calories, 7 g fat, 500 mg sodium.

Bulgur Burger
• PAT HUMPHREY

- 2 cups bulgur wheat
- 2 cups water
- 1 cup walnuts
- ½ medium onion, quartered

- 1 clove garlic
- 1 teaspoon chicken-style seasoning
- 1 teaspoon salt

Place bulgur wheat in saucepan. Place remaining ingredients in blender and process until smooth. Pour over bulgur wheat and cook over low heat for about 5 minutes, stirring frequently. Turn off heat and let stand for 20 minutes. Spread evenly on cookie sheet and bake at 250° F for an hour or until dry. Freeze and keep on hand to use for enchiladas, pizza, tacos, or burgers.
Makes 12 servings. 98 calories, 2 g fat, 183 mg sodium.

Vegetable Rice 1
• PAT HUMPHREY

- 2 cups Uncle Ben's 30 minute rice
- 2 tablespoons oil
- 1 4-ounce can tomato sauce
- 2½ cups water
- ½ teaspoon salt
- 1 clove garlic, minced
- 1 teaspoon McKay's Chicken Style Seasoning
- 1 8-ounce package frozen mixed vegetables

Stir-fry rice in oil about 10 minutes. Add tomato sauce, water, and seasonings; stir. Simmer for about 10 minutes, then add vegetables.
Makes 8 servings. 316 calories, 6.5 g fat, 177 mg sodium.

Spanish Rice
• PAT HUMPHREY

- 1 medium onion, chopped
- 1 small green pepper, diced
- 1 clove garlic, minced
- 1 cup canned tomatoes
- 1 teaspoon salt
- 2 cups Uncle Ben's 30-minute brown rice
- 4 cups water
- ½ cup sliced olives

Sauté onion, green pepper, and garlic in a heavy pan in a small amount of water until tender. Add next four ingredients and boil rapidly for 5 minutes. Reduce heat and simmer 25 minutes. Turn heat off and let stand 10 minutes. Add ½ cup sliced olives and serve.

Makes 8 servings. 218 calories, 1.4 g fat, 263 mg sodium.

Mexican Rice

• PAT HUMPHREY

    1½ cups brown rice
     3 tablespoons oil
     1 large onion, chopped
     ½ chili seeded and chopped
     2 cloves garlic, chopped
     4 tomatoes, peeled and chopped
     1 cup carrot, peeled and chopped
     3 cups vegetable stock
     1 can enchilada sauce
     ¾ cup frozen peas
       Salt, to taste
       Cilantro, chopped

Put rice in a heat proof bowl, cover with boiling water, and let sit for 10 minutes; drain thoroughly. Heat oil in a pan, add rice, and fry over low heat, stirring constantly, for about five minutes. Add chopped onion, chili, garlic, tomatoes, and carrots to pan and continue to cook for a minute or so. Add stock and enchilada sauce and bring to a boil. Stir rice well, cover (use glass lid, if possible), and simmer over low heat for 20 minutes (or until water is almost absorbed) without lifting lid. Stir in peas and continue cooking five minutes more, or until liquid is absorbed and rice is tender. Let covered pan sit for 5 to 10 additional minutes, then fork up rice and serve garnished with chopped cilantro.

Makes 6 servings. 462 calories, 16 g fat, 1,162 mg sodium.

Black Bean Spread

• PAT HUMPHREY

     1 16-ounce can black beans
     ½ teaspoon garlic powder
     ½ teaspoon onion powder
     ½ teaspoon cumin powder
       Dash of chili powder
       Salt to taste

Mash beans thoroughly and add seasonings. Great on pita bread or with tortilla chips!

Makes 16 servings. 25 calories, less than 1 g fat and sodium (without salt).

Tortilla Pizza

• CHRISTINA FLEMING-GABRIEL

     2 flour tortillas
     ¼ scant cup plain spaghetti sauce
     1 ounce soy cheese, mozzarella style

Preheat oven to 350° F. In cast-iron skillet, lightly brown tortillas on both sides and then place on a cookie sheet. Top tortillas with spaghetti sauce and mozzarella cheese. Bake for 15 minutes until cheese is melted and tortillas are crispy.

Makes 2 servings. 199 calories, 7.7 g fat, 435 mg sodium.

Soft Tacos de Soya

• PAMELA WILLIAMS

     8 ounces firm tofu
     1 onion, chopped
     2 cloves garlic, chopped
     2 tablespoons low-sodium soy sauce
     1 teaspoon chili powder
     ¼ teaspoon cumin
     1 large tomato, chopped
    12 corn tortillas

Prepare the following garnishes ahead of time: chopped tomatoes, shredded lettuce, chopped black olives, guacamole, and picante sauce. Crumble tofu with fingers. Spray large frying pan with vegetable cooking spray. Place on a low heat and sauté onions and garlic for 1 minute or until onions are tender. Add tofu and stir constantly for 1 minute. Add soy sauce, chili, and cumin; stir for an additional minute. Add tomatoes, cover and cook 5 minutes longer, stirring occasionally. Remove from heat. Spray another frying pan lightly with vegetable cooking spray and place on medium heat. Place each tortilla in frying pan for 30 seconds, flip tortilla over for additional 30 seconds. Fold tortilla in half; add tofu filling and other garnishes as desired. Serve.

Makes 6 servings: 164 calories, 9 g fat, 530 mg sodium.

Tomato Salsa (Mexico)
• PAT HUMPHREY

    4 ripe, firm red tomatoes
    1 medium red-skinned onion
  1-2 cloves garlic, crushed
    2 tablespoons fresh cilantro, chopped
    1 tablespoon No-Alarm Chili Powder (p. 100)
    ¼ lemon rind, grated
    2 tablespoons lemon or lime juice

Chop tomatoes finely and put into bowl. Peel and slice red onion thinly. Add to tomatoes with garlic, cilantro, and No-Alarm Chili Powder. Mix lightly. Add lemon or lime rind and juice; mix well. Transfer to serving bowl. To store, cover with plastic wrap and place in refrigerator.

Makes 6 servings. 23 calories, 0 g fat, 6 mg sodium.

Salt-free Salsa
• JOCELYN M. PETERSON

    2 medium tomatoes, chopped (about 2 cups)
    2 tablespoons sweet relish
    2 teaspoons minced red bell pepper
    2 tablespoons fresh lime juice
       Medium onion, chopped
    1 clove garlic, minced
    1 teaspoon honey
    1 tablespoon dried parsley

In a small bowl, mix all ingredients. Serve immediately. Leftover salsa can be refrigerated in a well-sealed container for three to four days. To peel the tomatoes, plunge them into boiling water for 30 seconds, then into cold water. The skins will slip off with ease.

10 calories, 0 g fat, 5 mg sodium.

Mexican Salsa
• PAT HUMPHREY

    3 cups canned tomatoes, crushed
    ½ cup bell pepper, chopped
    ¼ cup onion, chopped
    ¼ teaspoon garlic, crushed
    ½ teaspoon salt
    1 cup tomatos, chopped
    2 teaspoons fresh cilantro, chopped

Whiz tomatoes, bell peppers, onion, garlic, and salt in blender for 5 seconds. Stir in fresh chopped tomatoes and cilantro.

Makes 20 servings. 10 calories, less than 1 g fat, 56 mg sodium.

Side Dishes

If you're paying attention to the latest health trends, you've probably noticed a lot of talk about the importance of eating vegetables. What are people saying? The same thing our mothers told us all along: "Eat your vegetables." Recent scientific discoveries indicate that vegetables are not only high in vitamins and minerals, but also contain special compounds called phytochemicals that play a major role in preventing such diseases as diabetes, cancer, and heart disease. These recipes are dedicated to your health, happiness, and longevity. So eat and be healthy.

VEGETABLES

Eggplant Salad (Venezuela)
• PAMELA WILLIAMS

  1 large eggplant
     Salt
  3 tablespoons olive oil
  1 onion, chopped
  4 tomatoes, blanched, peeled, and chopped
     Pinch of raw sugar
     Cayenne pepper
20 small green or black olives
  1 pound green beans, cut into 1-inch pieces
  4 tablespoons lemon juice
  3 tablespoons parsley, chopped

Cut eggplant into 1-inch slices, then cut each slice into thin strips. Place strips in a bowl and sprinkle with salt. Let set for 30 minutes. Pour off liquid and rinse off salt. Pat dry with a paper towel. In a large skillet, add oil and sauté the onion and eggplant until both are soft. Add tomatoes, sugar, and pepper. Stir in olives and cook until liquid is somewhat dry. In the meantime, boil green beans in salted water in a saucepan. Cook until tender, about 7 minutes. Drain and chill. Toss green beans with lemon juice and parsley. Place eggplant in the middle of a serving platter and surround eggplant with green beans.
Makes 6 servings. 139 calories, 8.5 g fat, 282 mg sodium.

Summer Squash With Bell Pepper
• JOCELYN M. PETERSON

  ½ medium sliced onion
  1 cup thinly sliced red and green bell peppers
  1 tablespoon olive oil
  3 medium-sized summer squash, thinly sliced
  1 tablespoon dried parsley
  1 teaspoon cumin
  1 tablespoon garlic powder
  1 tablespoon McKay's Chicken Style Seasoning

Sauté onions and red and green bell peppers in olive oil for 3 minutes. Add sliced squash and seasonings. Simmer for 3 minutes. Do not overcook.
Makes 4 servings. 60 calories, 3 g fat, 15 mg sodium.

Side Dish Tips

• Try adding dried fruit, nuts, or chopped vegetables (such as green onions, garlic, broccoli, or others) to your next batch of rice. It will give the dish extra punch and texture.

• Cooking vegetables too much will make them mushy and tasteless. Cook until they are still a bit crispy, and they'll taste better and retain more of their vitamins and nutrition, too.

• Create non-traditional type side dishes like stuffing or fresh fruit to add variety to your weekday meals.

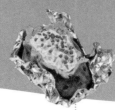

Orange Acorn Squash

• PAMELA AND ERMA WILLIAMS

   2 acorn squash
   1 tablespoon butter
   2 cups orange juice
   1 teaspoon orange rind
      Salt to taste

Quarter each squash. Peel and remove seeds. Steam squash until tender. Set aside. In a skillet, combine the melted butter, orange juice, honey, and salt. Bring to a boil and simmer for 3 minutes. Place squash in a baking dish. Pour the syrup over the squash. Garnish with orange peel.
Makes 4 servings. 124 calories, 3 g fat.

Baked Acorn Squash With Apple Stuffing

• DONNA A. SMITH

   2 medium acorn squash
   4 small apples, unpeeled, diced
  ¼ cup diced celery
   4 teaspoons margarine, melted
  ¼ cup apple juice
  ¼ teaspoon salt

Preheat oven to 400° F. Cut squash in half. Remove seeds and place cut side down on baking sheet sprayed with vegetable pan spray. Combine apples and celery in a bowl. Add margarine and apple juice. Place in small baking dish and cover. Bake both squash and apple stuffing for 45 minutes, or until tender. Remove from oven. Salt squash and fill with apple mixture. Serve.
Makes 4 servings. 181 calories, 5 g fat, 305 mg sodium.

Candied Yams

• PAT HUMPHREY

   6 yams, peeled and cooked
   1 cup maple syrup
   1 bag kosher marshmallows

Slice yams into casserole dish lightly sprayed with nonstick coating. Pour maple syrup over yams, top with marshmallows, and bake at 350° F until bubbly.
Makes 8 servings. 250 calories, 1 g fat, 175 mg sodium.

Curried Calabaza

• PAMELA WILLIAMS

   2 tablespoons vegetable oil
   1 medium onion, chopped
   2 garlic cloves, chopped
   2 tablespoons curry powder
   2 cardamom pods seeds, ground
  ½ teaspoon ground allspice
   1 red bell pepper, seeded and diced
   1 bay leaf, crushed
   2 medium tomatoes, blanched, peeled, and chopped
1½ pounds calabaza or winter squash, peeled, seeded, and cut into cubes
   1 cup water
   1 teaspoon McKay's Chicken Style Seasoning
  ¼ teaspoon of salt or salt to taste

In a large nonstick heavy skillet heat oil over medium heat. Add onion, garlic, and curry powder. Cook until onion is wilted. Add cardamom, all-spice, bell pepper, and bay leaf. Cook 2 more minutes. Add tomatoes, squash, water, McKay's Chicken Style Seasoning, and salt. Cover and cook over very low heat for 25 minutes or until squash is tender. Add a little more water if mixture thickens. Serve immediately.
Makes 6 servings. 88 calories, 5 g fat, 98 mg sodium.

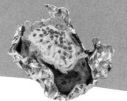

Mexi-corn

• JOCELYN M. PETERSON

- 1 pound frozen or fresh corn kernels
- 1 cup chopped red bell peppers
- 1 teaspoon garlic powder
- 1 teaspoon cumin
- 1 tablespoon dry parsley
- 1 tablespoon olive oil

Sauté all above ingredients in olive oil. Serve hot.

Makes 5 servings. 50 calories, 3 g fat, 20 mg sodium.

Grilled Vegetables

• PAMELA AND ERMA WILLIAMS

- ¼ cup oil
- 2 tablespoons water
- 1 tablespoon lime juice
- 3 cloves garlic, crushed
- 2 teaspoons fresh thyme, chopped
- ¼ teaspoon salt or salt to taste
- 2 medium onions, sliced 3 inches thick
- 2 small eggplants, halved lengthwise
- 1 chayote, halved lengthwise and cored
- 12 shiitake mushroom caps, halved
- 2 red, yellow, or green bell peppers, seeded and cut in strips
- 6 Russet potatoes with skins, sliced ½ inch thick

Combine oil, water, lime juice, garlic, thyme, and salt in a small bowl. Put the vegetables in a dish and pour mixture on top. Marinate at room temperature for 1 hour. Thread six skewers, alternating vegetables. Place on cookie sheet and broil for 10 minutes until done. Turn as vegetables brown. Serve warm with protein dish or serve alone. Another alternative is to grill vegetables at a picnic.

Makes 6 servings. 252 calories, 7 g fat, 106 mg sodium.

Stir-fry Vegetable Medley (Oriental)

• PAMELA AND ERMA WILLIAMS

- 1-2 cups water
- 8 ounces fresh green beans, cut into one-inch pieces
- 2 fresh carrots, cut into thin diagonal pieces
  Nonstick cooking spray
- 1 clove garlic, minced
- 1 medium onion, cut into thin slices and halved
- 8 ounces fresh mushrooms, cut into slices
- 1 teaspoon light soy sauce
- ½ teaspoons McKay's Chicken Style Seasoning
- ¼ cups water

Bring water to boil in a saucepan. Add beans and carrots. Cover and simmer for 7 to 10 minutes and drain. In a skillet sauté garlic, onions, and mushrooms on low heat until tender. In a small bowl, combine McKay's Chicken-Style Seasoning, soy sauce, and water, and add mixture to skillet. Stir in beans and carrots, and cook for three minute or until vegetables are crisp. Serve.

Makes 6 servings. 34 calories, 0 g fat.

Italian Stir-fry Green Beans (Italy)

• CHRISTINA FLEMING GABRIEL

- 2 tablespoons vegetable oil
- 1 pound fresh string beans, parboiled
- ½ teaspoon each: garlic powder, basil, oregano, and crushed red pepper
- ¼ cup Italian salad dressing
- 1 teaspoon salt (optional)

In a large frying pan, heat vegetable oil over a medium-high flame. Add string beans, garlic powder, basil, oregano, and crushed red pepper. Stir frequently to prevent burning. Once string beans are tender, add salad dressing. Mix salad dressing with string beans until beans are well coated and salad dressing is heating. Remove from heat and serve.

Makes 5 servings. 83 calories, 5.2 g fat, 169 mg sodium.

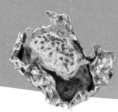

Cabbage and Onions
• PAMELA AND ERMA WILLIAMS

- 1 tablespoon oil
- 1 pound cabbage, shredded
- 1 large onion, sliced
- ½ teaspoon salt
- Dash of cayenne
- 2 tablespoons water

Sauté cabbage and onion in oil. Add water and seasonings. Simmer covered for about 10 minutes or until tender. Stir occasionally.
Makes 4 servings. 51 calories, 3.5 g fat, 295 mg sodium.

Mustard Greens
• PAMELA AND IRMA WILLIAMS

- 6 Worthington® Stripples®, broken into pieces
- 2 tablespoons olive oil
- 1 onion, sliced into rings
- 1½ pounds of mustard greens, washed and stems removed, cut into pieces
- ½ teaspoon chicken-style seasoning
- 2-3 cups water

Spray heavy skillet with non-stick vegetable spray and sauté Stripples®. Add olive oil and mustard greens. Sauté for two minutes and add water. Cook until tender.
Makes 4 servings. 120 calories, 5.5 g fat, 424 mg sodium.

Seasoned Collards
• JOCELYN M. PETERSON

- 2 cups chopped or sliced onions
- 1 chopped red bell pepper
- 2 tablespoons olive oil
- 2 pounds collard greens, washed (well chopped, as desired)
- ½ cup water
- 3 tablespoons Mrs. Dash seasoning (optional)

Sauté onions, peppers, and oil together in large saucepan. Add chopped greens and water. Cover. Cook slowly, stirring frequently until done (20-30 minutes).
Makes 6 servings. 60 calories, trace fat, 0.5 mg sodium.

Mean Greens
• BARBARA FRAZIER

- 1 pound collard greens (kale or spinach)
- Olive oil cooking spray
- 1 teaspoon garlic powder
- 1 lemon, juiced and seeded
- 2 teaspoons Fakin' Bacon Bits

Wash greens 2 or 3 times in cold water. Remove large stems and discolored leaves. Place skillet on stove and spray generously with cooking spray. Roll several leaves of greens into tight roll. Using cutting board, thinly slice greens crosswise. Transfer greens to skillet. Sprinkle evenly with garlic powder and lemon juice. Stir-fry quickly for about 3 minutes, adding cooking spray and water as needed. Remove from heat and sprinkle with Fakin' Bacon Bits. Cover briefly before serving.
Makes 4 servings. 23 calories, 2 g fat, 2 g protein, 38 mg sodium.

Ethiopian Collard Greens (Africa)
• PAT HUMPHREY

- 1 pound collard greens
- 4 tablespoons olive oil
- 2 small red onions, finely chopped
- 1 clove garlic, crushed
- ½ teaspoon ginger, grated
- 2 green chilies, seeded and sliced
- ⅔ cup Vegetable Stock (p. 38)
- 1 red bell pepper, seeded and sliced
- Salt

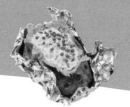

Wash greens, then strip the leaves from stalks and steam in steamer for about five minutes, until slightly wilted. Set aside to cool, then place greens in strainer or colander and press out excess water. Using a large, sharp knife, slice the greens thinly. Heat oil in a saucepan and fry the onions until browned. Add garlic and ginger and stir-fry with onions a few minutes, then add chilies and a little stock and cook for 2 minutes. Add greens, red pepper, and remaining stock. Season with salt, mix well, then cover and cook for about 15 minutes.
Makes 4 servings. 208 calories, 15 g fat, 292 mg sodium.

Collards and Corn Patties
• PAMELA AND ERMA WILLIAMS

  1 large bunch fresh collard greens
  ½ teaspoon salt
  1 teaspoon honey
  1 tablespoon oil
  6 Worthington® Stripples
  1 cup cornmeal

Wash and remove stems from collard greens. Cut up and place in pot. Add salt, honey, oil, and enough water to make plenty of liquid. Cook until tender. Crumble Stripples into collard greens. Combine cornmeal, salt, and enough liquid from collard greens to shape into patties. Drop patties into boiling collard greens. Make sure there is enough liquid to cover patties and greens. Cook until tender.
Makes 4 servings. 236 calories, 7.5 g fat, 468 mg sodium.

Green Vegetables With Coconut Milk (Uganda)
• PAT HUMPHREY

  1 onion, chopped
  2 pounds spinach or kale
  1 cup coconut milk
    Salt
    Red bell pepper, sliced

Cover the bottom of a saucepan with water and bring it to a boil. Add onion and allow to cook a few minutes; then add green vegetable. Cover and simmer for 5 minutes, then add coconut milk, season, and stir. Cook uncovered for 20 minutes more. Serve hot, and garnish with red bell pepper slices.
Makes 4 servings. 188 calories, 15 g fat, 139 mg sodium.

Mushroom and Vegetable Casserole
• PAMELA AND ERMA WILLIAMS

  1 cup cooked string beans
  1 cup cooked carrots
  1 onion, chopped
  ½ cup chopped mushrooms
  1 cup cooked corn
  1 cup cooked peas
  1 cup mushroom soup
  1 cup Italian seasoned bread crumbs
    Parmesan cheese

Mix vegetables together. Place a layer of mixed vegetables in oiled casserole dish. Cover with layer of mushroom soup. Repeat until dish is nearly filled. Dust with 1 cup bread crumbs and sprinkle with Parmesan cheese. Bake for 30 minutes in a 400° F oven until brown.
Makes 10 servings. 93 calories, 1.5 g fat.

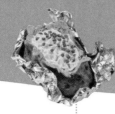

Sautéed Eggplant Rounds in Pasta Sauce

• BARBARA FRAZIER

    1 firm eggplant
       Basil, oregano, garlic powder to taste
    3 tablespoons water
    3 cups pasta sauce

Wash eggplant and pat dry. Place skillet on the stove and spray with olive oil cooking spray. Slice unpeeled eggplant in ⅜-inch rounds into skillet, arranging in staggered layers. Sprinkle with seasonings to taste. Add a little water as needed. Cover skillet and sauté three minutes. Carefully turn eggplant over with spatula. Sprinkle face up side with seasonings. Pour pasta sauce over eggplant evenly. Cover and sauté for three more minutes. Spoon eggplant and sauce over prepared linguine pasta. Makes 6 servings. 54 calories, 3 g fat, 1 g protein, 108 mg sodium.
COOK'S HINT: Prego Roasted Garlic and Herb Pasta Sauce works well.

Curried Eggplant (India)

• PAMELA WILLIAMS

    2 large eggplants, peeled and cubed
    1 teaspoon salt
    2 large onions, chopped
    2 garlic cloves, chopped
    ½ teaspoon cumin
    1 teaspoon coriander
    ½ teaspoon cardamom
    2 teaspoons fresh ginger, grated
    ½ teaspoon turmeric
    1 teaspoon nutmeg
       Dash of cayenne pepper
    1 tablespoon oil
    3 tablespoons water
    3 large potatoes, chopped
    2 tomatoes, blanched, peeled, and chopped
    1 teaspoon tomato paste
    ½ package frozen spinach
    1½ cups water

Sprinkle eggplant chunks with salt and set aside for 10 minutes. Spray a large skillet with vegetable oil and sauté onions and garlic until tender. Mix and grind spices together and add to skillet. Stir for 2-3 minutes. Rinse salt off eggplant pieces and pat with paper towels to get rid of excess moisture. Add eggplant, oil, and water to the skillet. Stir until eggplant is tender. Add potatoes and let brown. Add tomatoes, tomato paste, spinach, and 1½ cups water. Stir to keep from sticking and bring mixture to a boil. Reduce and simmer until vegetables are tender and crisp and sauce is thick. Serve on a bed of brown rice or millet.
Makes 6 servings. 135 calories, 1 g fat, 231 mg sodium.

Grits 'n' Vegetables

• PAMELA AND ERMA WILLIAMS

    ⅔ cup grits
    3 cups water
    ¼ teaspoon salt
    1 red onion, chopped
    2 garlic cloves, minced
    ½ bell pepper
    2 teaspoons olive oil
    1 eggplant, unpeeled and cut into cubes
    ¼ cup water
    ¼ teaspoon salt
    1 zucchini, halved and thinly sliced crosswise
    1 8-ounce can tomato sauce
    2 tablespoons fresh basil, chopped
    1 tablespoon fresh oregano, chopped

Preheat oven to 400° F. Cook grits in 3 cups water and ¼ teaspoon salt. When thick, spoon into a 9-inch square baking dish and set aside. Saute onions, bell pepper, and garlic in oil until soft. Stir in eggplant, toss, and add ⅓ cup water and ¼ teaspoon salt. Cover and cook until eggplant is tender. Stir in zucchini, tomato sauce, and herbs. Cook until sauce is lightly thickened. Spoon mixture over grits and bake until hot—about 10 minutes.
Makes 4 servings. 102 calories, 3.5 g fat, 295 mg sodium.

Okra, Corn, and Tomatoes
• PAMELA AND ERMA WILLIAMS

   1 medium onion, chopped
   ½ medium bell pepper, chopped
   1 teaspoon olive oil
   ½ pound okra sliced into half-inch slices
   1 15-ounce can tomatoes, chopped
   1 15-ounce can whole kernel corn, drained
   ½ teaspoon basil
   ¼ teaspoon oregano

Sauté onion and bell pepper in olive oil until soft. Add okra and cook 5 minutes, stirring with wooden spoon. Add tomatoes, corn, and herbs. Stir. Lower heat and cook an additional 10 minutes. Serve immediately.
Makes 6 servings. 108 calories, 0.5 g fat, 226 mg sodium.

Corn Chowder
• PAT HUMPHREY

   3 cups water
   2 cups diced potatoes
   2 teaspoons onion powder
   ½ teaspoon celery salt
   2 cups canned corn
   2 cups water
   ½ cup raw cashews
   2 tablespoons cornstarch

Cook first 5 ingredients until the vegetables are tender. Meanwhile, blend the remaining ingredients until smooth. Add the blended mixture to the vegetables and simmer 10-15 minutes. Salt to taste. Serve hot.
Makes 6 servings. 249 calories, 10.4 g fat, 89 mg sodium.

Okra and Tomatoes
• PAT HUMPHREY

   1 medium onion, chopped
   1 small green pepper, chopped
   1 clove garlic, chopped
   1 tablespoon cooking oil
   3 large tomatoes, peeled
     Salt to taste
   2 pounds okra, ends trimmed
     Fresh parsley, chopped

Cook onion, green pepper, and garlic in oil over low heat about 10 minutes. Add tomatoes and salt and mix well. Add okra and simmer for 30 minutes. Pour into a serving dish and garnish with chopped parsley.
Makes 6 servings. 87 calories, 2.7 g fat, 344 mg sodium.

Okra and Tomatoes With Rice
• CHRISTINA FLEMING GABRIEL

   1 tablespoon vegetable oil
   1 medium chopped onion
   1 10-ounce package frozen chopped okra, thawed
   4 chopped plum tomatoes
   ½ teaspoon each: garlic powder, basil, oregano, and crushed red pepper
  1½ cups cooked brown rice

In a large frying pan over medium heat, add oil and onion. Sauté chopped onion until translucent. Add chopped okra, plum tomatoes, garlic powder, basil, oregano, and crushed red pepper. Cook until tomatoes release juices and are tender. Stirring frequently, add rice and cook until rice is heated thoroughly. Remove from heat and serve.
Makes 4 servings. 158 calories, 3.7 g fat, 267 mg sodium.

Honeyed Carrots
• DONNA GREEN GOODMAN

  2 pounds fresh carrots, peeled and sliced
  ¼ cup honey

Place sliced carrots in saucepan in ½ cup water. Bring to boil and let boil for about 5 minutes uncovered. Pour honey over carrots and cover. Turn to low and let steam till crisp tender.
Makes 8 servings. 81 calories, less than 1 g fat, 40 mg sodium.

Carrot and Green Bean Curry
• PAT HUMPHREY

  1 tablespoon safflower oil
  1 large yellow onion, minced
  ½ piece ginger root, minced
  1 clove garlic, minced
  1 teaspoon turmeric
  1 teaspoon curry powder
  1 tomato, diced (or ½ cup stewed tomatoes)
  3 carrots, sliced diagonally
  ½ pound green beans, cut in 2-inch diagonal slices

Stir-fry onion, ginger root, and garlic in oil, using wok or skillet over medium high heat, for 5-10 minutes. Add turmeric, curry powder, and tomatoes and simmer for 2 minutes. Stir in carrots and beans; cook 5 minutes. Simmer covered on low heat for 15 minutes or until vegetables are tender. Stir often.
Makes 6 servings. 64 calories, 3 g fat, 17 mg sodium.

Peas and Lettuce
• JOCELYN M. PETERSON

  6 outer leaves of lettuce (Boston, Cobb, etc.)
  1 small onion or shallot, sliced
  2 tablespoons olive oil
  8 ounces fresh or frozen peas
  1 tablespoon McKay's Chicken Style Seasoning
  1 tablespoon garlic powder

Pull off the outer lettuce leaves and wash them well. Roughly shred the leaves with your hands. In a saucepan, lightly fry the lettuce and onion or shallot in the olive oil for 3 minutes. Add peas, McKay's Chicken Style Seasoning, and garlic powder. Stir; cover and simmer for about 5 minutes. This dish can be drained or served slightly wet.
Makes 4 servings. 60 calories, 3 g fat, 10 mg sodium.

Snow Peas With Carrots and Red Pepper
• PAT HUMPHREY

     Vegetable cooking spray
  1 tablespoon unsalted margarine
  2 medium carrots, cut into matchstick strips
  1 medium sweet red pepper, cut into matchstick strips
  ¾ pound snow peas
  ¼ teaspoon grated lemon rind
  1 teaspoon lemon juice

Coat a heavy skillet or wok with cooking spray. Add margarine and melt it over medium heat. Add carrots and red pepper and cook, covered, for 3 minutes. Add snow peas, cover, and cook 3 minutes longer or until vegetables are tender. Stir in lemon rind and lemon juice.
Makes 4 servings. 83 calories, 3 g fat, 17 mg sodium.

Spicy Glazed Carrots
• PAT HUMPHREY

  ¾ cup water
  8 medium carrots, peeled and sliced diagonally
  ¾ teaspoon ground cumin
  ½ teaspoon ground ginger
  ¼ teaspoon ground coriander
  ⅛ teaspoon ground cayenne pepper
  2 teaspoons honey
  2 teaspoons lemon juice

Bring water to boil in a heavy 10-inch skillet. Add carrots, cumin, ginger, coriander, and cayenne.

Cover, reduce heat, and simmer for 12 minutes. Add honey and lemon juice and cook until liquid has evaporated and carrots are tender (about 4 minutes).

Makes 4 servings. 58 calories, 0 g fat, 37 mg sodium.

Orange Glazed Carrots
• DONNA A. SMITH

½ cup water
½ teaspoon salt
2½ cups sliced carrots
½ cup unsweetened orange juice
1 tablespoon cornstarch
1 medium orange, diced
2 tablespoons brown sugar, or to taste

Bring salted water to a boil. Add carrots. Cover and cook until tender. Drain the liquid into a measuring cup and add orange juice. Add enough water to make 1 cup of liquid. Remove carrots from pan. In saucepan mix liquid with cornstarch. Cook, stirring constantly until mixture thickens. Add margarine, brown sugar, and oranges and heat.

Makes 6 servings. 101 calories, 4 g fat, 252 mg sodium.

Sesame Broccoli
• PAT HUMPHREY

1 pound fresh broccoli
1 tablespoon canola oil
1 tablespoon lemon juice
1 tablespoon soy sauce
4 teaspoons honey
1 tablespoon toasted sesame seed

Steam broccoli until tender. Combine other ingredients in saucepan and heat to boiling. Pour sauce over hot broccoli, turning spears to coat. Serve immediately.

Makes 6 servings. 66 calories, 3.7 g fat, 152 mg sodium.

Broccoli Lo Mein
• CHRISTINA FLEMING GREEN

2 tablespoons vegetable oil
1 10-ounce package frozen broccoli thawed (or leftover cooked broccoli)
1 large onion, chopped
½ teaspoon each: garlic powder, basil, oregano, and crushed red pepper
1 tablespoon soy sauce, lite
1 cup hot tap water
1 tablespoon cornstarch
 Salt (optional)

Over medium-high heat in a large skillet, add oil, broccoli, and onions. Add garlic powder, basil oregano, and crushed red pepper. Stir frequently to prevent burning. Once broccoli is almost tender, mix thoroughly in a large measuring cup the soy sauce, water, and cornstarch and pour over the broccoli stir-fry mixture, incorporating thoroughly. Heat sauce until it thickens. Remove from heat and serve over pasta.

Makes 4 servings. 96 calories, 6 g fat, 142 mg sodium.

Side Dishes

Sesame Green Beans
• PAT HUMPHREY

> 1 pound green beans
> 2 tablespoons chunky peanut butter
> 1 tablespoon sesame oil
> 1 teaspoon soy sauce
> ¼ teaspoon cayenne
> 1 teaspoon honey
> 2 tablespoons lemon juice

Add beans to a large pot of boiling water. Add salt to taste, and cook beans for about 5 or 6 minutes. Drain and rinse. Mix peanut butter, sesame oil, and soy sauce in a large bowl. Add cayenne, honey, and lemon juice to mixture. Toss in beans and stir until coated with dressing. Chill.
Makes 4 servings. 97 calories, 6 g fat, 90 mg sodium.

Tropical Vegetables In Coconut Milk (West Indies)
• PAT HUMPHREY

> 1 tablespoon canola oil
> 1 teaspoon garlic, minced
> 1 red chili pepper, seeded and sliced
> 2 cups coconut milk
> 2½ pounds yams or other starchy vegetables, peeled and diced
> 1 pound butternut squash
> 1 cup plum tomatoes, finely chopped
> 1 tablespoon mild curry powder
> 1 teaspoon salt

Saute garlic in oil over medium-high heat, stirring constantly until lightly browned. Add chili pepper, coconut milk, starchy vegetables (such as yams, cassava, yucca, taro, etc.), butternut squash, tomatoes, curry powder, and salt. Cook on medium heat for about 30 minutes or until vegetables are tender. Stir well before serving. Serve over brown rice along with a steamed green vegetable. (For a nonirritating healthy alternative, use Bill's Best Curry Powder, available from health food stores or from Sovex (423-396-3145). Starchy vegetables can be purchased in some grocery stores or in West Indian or Latino markets.)
Makes 6 servings. 309 calories, 17 g fat, 378 mg sodium.

Italian Zucchini (Italy)
• PAMELA AND ERMA WILLIAMS

> 4 zucchinis, cut into ½ inch slices
> 2 tomatoes, blanched, peeled, and quartered
> 1 onion, sliced
> 2 tablespoons oil
> ½ teaspoon garlic
> ½ teaspoon oregano

Sauté onion and garlic in oil. Add zucchini and 2 tablespoons water. Cover and simmer for 2 minutes. Add the rest of the ingredients and cool for 1-2 minutes before serving.
Makes 6 servings. 129 calories, 6 g fat.

Zucchini Patties
• PAT HUMPHREY

> 1 cup Tofu Mayonnaise 4 (p. 51)
> 2 cups bread crumbs
> 3 cups shredded zucchini
> 1 teaspoon onion powder
> ½ teaspoon garlic powder
> 1 teaspoon salt
> ⅛ teaspoon tarragon
> ⅛ teaspoon marjoram
> ⅛ teaspoon thyme
> ⅛ teaspoon ground celery leaves
> ⅛ teaspoon ground bay leaves

Mix all ingredients, varying the seasonings according to taste. Shape mixture into patties and brown them in a pan lightly coated with vegetable spray.
Makes 12 servings. 50 calories, 0.6 g fat, 416 mg sodium.

POTATOES, RICE, AND DRESSINGS

Mashed Red Potatoes and Onions
• JOCELYN M. PETERSON

    12 red potatoes
    ½ cup hot nonfat milk
    ½ teaspoon salt
     4 onions, sliced thin
    ½ teaspoon powdered sage

Wash potatoes; steam in their skins until tender. Cut potatoes into large squares with skins on and then mash with hot milk and salt. Spray skillet with nonstick vegetable spray and sauté onions until golden brown. Sprinkle with sage and salt. Add to potatoes.
Makes 4 servings. 181 calories, 0 g fat, 302 mg sodium.

Cheesy Mashed Potatoes
• DONNA A. SMITH

     2 pounds medium potatoes (about 6)
     1 tablespoon margarine
     1 cup plain tofu yogurt
    ¾ cup almond/rice shredded cheddar cheese
    ¼ teaspoon salt
    ¼ teaspoon cayenne pepper

Cover and cook potatoes in boiling salted water 30 minutes, or until tender. Drain, then add margarine and mash potatoes. Combine with yogurt and whip until light and fluffy. Stir in cheese, salt, and pepper.
Makes 6 servings. 212 calories, 3 g fat, 277 mg sodium.

Mashed Potatoes
• DONNA GREEN GOODMAN

     3 pounds white potatoes
    ½ cup soy milk
    ¾ teaspoon salt
     1 teaspoon McCormick garlic and herb flavored seasoning
     2 teaspoons McKay's Chicken Style Seasoning (no MSG)
     1 teaspoon nutritional yeast flakes
    ½ teaspoon garlic powder
    ½ teaspoon onion powder
        Paprika
        Parsley, chopped

Peel and boil potatoes in a small amount of water. When tender, keep about a fourth of the boiled water in potatoes, add other ingredients, and mash. Garnish with paprika and chopped parsley.
Makes 8 servings. 147 calories, less than 1 gram fat, 142 mg sodium.

Garlicky Mashed Potatoes
• PAMELA AND ERMA WILLIAMS

     3 pounds potatoes, peeled and cubed
     6 cloves garlic
    ¼ cup nonfat milk
     1 tablespoon butter
    22 tablespoons chopped parsley
        Salt
     6 tablespoons skim milk
        Mozzarella cheese

Boil potatoes for 20 minutes or until tender. Drain and cool. Meanwhile, in a small saucepan, bring peeled garlic cloves to a boil in a small amount of water and then simmer for 15 minutes. Drain and cool. Combine milk and garlic in a blender or food processor. Puree. Mash potatoes with an electric mixer and add pureed garlic, butter, chopped parsley, and salt to taste. Add milk as needed to achieve a smooth texture. Garnish with mozzarella cheese and serve.
Makes 6 servings. 215 calories, 4 g fat.

Scalloped Potatoes

• PAT HUMPHREY

- 1 pound white potatoes, thinly sliced
- 1 cup raw cashews
- 2 cups water
- 2 teaspoons salt
- 1 teaspoon onion powder
- Paprika

Place potatoes in a glass casserole dish. Blend remaining ingredients in blender, then pour over potatoes. Cover with aluminum foil and bake for 1 hour at 375° F. Remove foil, sprinkle with paprika, and return potatoes to oven for about 5 minutes or until lightly browned.
Makes 6 servings. 210 calories, 14 g fat, 502 mg sodium.

Capricorn Hot Pot (Australia)

• PAT HUMPHREY

- 10 ounces corn, fresh or frozen
- ½ pound green beans diced
- 10 ounces green peas, fresh or frozen
- 2 medium carrots, sliced
- 1 medium parsnip, sliced
- 1½ pounds potatoes, halved
- 1 tablespoon salad oil
- 1 cube vegetable bouillon
- ½ cup soy milk
- 1 tablespoon tamari soy sauce

Steam first five vegetables together until almost done. Steam the potatoes in a separate pot. Peel and cube two thirds of the potatoes and add to other vegetables. Place this mixture in a casserole dish. Peel and mash remaining potatoes with bouillon cube, soy sauce, soy silk, oil, and tamari. Top the vegetable mixture with mashed potatoes. Bake at 350° F about 20-25 minutes.
Makes 6 servings. 208 calories, 4 g fat, 196 mg sodium.

Oven Taters

• PAMELA AND ERMA WILLIAMS

- 4-5 potatoes, peeled
- Pam spray
- Salt to taste

Slice potatoes lengthwise into ½-inch strips. Soak strips in ice water for 20 minutes. Drain and dry thoroughly with paper towels. Place potatoes in a single layer on a baking sheet. Spray potatoes lightly with Pam. Preheat oven to 450° F and bake potatoes for 20 minutes. Turn and spray with Pam. Bake 20 minutes longer. Sprinkle lightly with salt.
Makes 2 servings: 176 calories, 1 g fat.

Potato and Cabbage Croquettes

• JOCELYN PETERSON

- 3 cups mashed potato
- 8 ounces steamed or boiled shredded cabbage
- 2 ounces egg substitute
- 2 ounces soy Parmesan cheese
- 1 tablespoon garlic powder
- 1 tablespoon dry parsley
- 1 teaspoon McKay's Chicken Style Seasoning
- 1 cup bread flour
- 1 tablespoon olive oil

Mix the potatoes with shredded cabbage, egg substitute, soy cheese, and seasonings. Divide and shape into eight croquettes. Chill for an hour or so, if possible, as this enables the mixture to become firm and makes it easier to fry. Toss the croquettes in the bread flour. Heat oil in a frying pan until it is quite hot. Carefully slide the croquettes into the oil and fry on each side for about 3 minutes until golden and crisp. Drain on paper towel and serve hot.
Makes 8 servings. 150 calories, 3 g fat, 50 mg sodium.

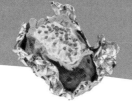

String Beans and Potatoes
• PAMELA AND ERMA WILLIAMS

    1 large onion, thinly sliced
    1 pound string beans
    4 potatoes, diced
    1 teaspoon salt
    1 cup boiling water
    2 teaspoons imitation bacon bits

Spray skillet with nonstick vegetable spray and sauté onion until brown. Add string beans, potatoes, salt, and water. Cover and simmer until tender. Add imitation bacon bits before serving.
Makes 6 servings. 106 calories, 0 g fat, 419 mg sodium.

Country Potato Patties
• PAMELA AND ERMA WILLIAMS

    2 potatoes, peeled and coarsely grated
    1 tablespoon minced onion
    ½ teaspoon flour
    ½ teaspoon salt

Combine ingredients. Shape into patties. Brown in 350° F oven on a cookie sheet sprinkled with cornmeal.
Makes 2 servings. 95 calories, 0 g fat.

Potato Patties
• PAT HUMPHREY

    4 cups mashed potatoes
    ½ cup fresh parsley, chopped
    1 tablespoon onion powder
    Paprika
    Salt

Mix potatoes, parsley, and onion powder together. (Cold, leftover mashed potatoes work well.) Shape into patties. Sprinkle with paprika and bake patties on cookie sheet sprayed with vegetable spray or brown patties in skillet.
Makes 6 servings. 94 calories, 1 g fat, 383 mg sodium.

Crispy Potato Skins (KIDS)
• PAMELA AND ERMA WILLIAMS

    2 large baking potatoes
    Nonstick cooking spray
    Seasoned salt
    Paprika

Preheat oven to 375° F. Prick the potatoes all over with a fork. Place on baking sheet and bake until outside is crisp—1½ hours. Cut potatoes in half and scoop out the inside to save for another use. Spray potatoes with cooking spray and sprinkle with seasoned salt and paprika. Return to oven for 5 to 10 minutes. Remove and cut into strips. Serve immediately.
Makes 4 servings. 50 calories, 1 g fat.

Sweet Potato Balls
• PAMELA AND ERMA WILLIAMS

    2 cups mashed cooked sweet potatoes
    2 tablespoons syrup
    Salt to taste
    ¼ teaspoon nutmeg
    ½ cup walnuts
    6 slices pineapple, drained
    1 tablespoon cream
    6 kosher marshmallows

Mix potatoes, syrup, salt, and nutmeg and form six balls. Place balls on pineapple, brush with cream. Bake 20 minutes at 350° F. Press marshmallows into the center of each ball and let brown for 5 minutes in the oven.
Makes 6 servings. 209 calories, 4.6 g fat.

Sweet Potatoes With Dates

• PAMELA WILLIAMS

  1 cup water
  ½ teaspoon cinnamon
  ¼ teaspoon cloves
  ½ pound pitted dates, chopped
  4 sweet potatoes, peeled and cut into cubes
  1 tablespoon butter
  ½ cup pineapple chunks
  1 cup water
  6 dried apricot halves
  ¼ cup walnuts, chopped

In a food processor, combine 1 cup water, cinnamon, cloves, and dates. Blend until smooth. In a large saucepan, add sweet potatoes and one tablespoon butter, and sauté over low heat for 1-2 minutes. Add pineapple cubes and cook until golden brown. Add blended dates and cook for an additional 5 minutes. Add 1 cup water and cook covered over a low to medium heat for 30 minutes. Mix in the dried apricots and cook for another 15 minutes or until sweet potatoes are tender. Remove and serve garnished with walnuts.
Makes 4 servings. 288 calories, 7 g fat, 14 mg sodium.

Crunchy Sweet Potatoes on Half Shell

• PAMELA AND ERMA WILLIAMS

  4 medium sweet potatoes
  ½ cup nonfat milk
  ½ teaspoon salt
  ¼ cup chopped pecans
  8 kosher marshmallows

Bake potatoes in a 400° F oven for 40 minutes or until soft. Remove potatoes and cool. Leave oven on. Cut potatoes in half lengthwise. Scoop out potatoes and mash. Beat in milk, salt, and pecans. Return mixture to shells. Top each with two marshmallows. Arrange on baking sheet and cook for five minutes. Marshmallows should melt and brown slightly.
Makes 8 servings. 95 calories, 1 g fat, 164 mg sodium.

Genovese Risotto (Italy)

• PAT HUMPHREY

  ¾ pound grated white cabbage
  3 pints vegetable stock
  1 pound brown rice
  1 tablespoon tomato paste
  ½ cup chopped nuts
  2 teaspoons salt or to taste

Cook the cabbage in vegetable stock for 6 minutes. Add the rice, and cook gently until done. Dilute the tomato paste in a little hot stock, and stir into the risotto. Add the chopped nuts, and season with salt.
Makes 10 servings. 219 calories, 6 g fat, 467 mg sodium.

Fancy Rice

• PAT HUMPHREY

  7 cups hot cooked brown rice, salted
  1 10-ounce package frozen peas, cooked
  3 tablespoons chopped pimiento

Press rice, peas, and pimiento into a six-cup ring mold. Unmold onto a 12-inch round serving platter. Place entrée of your choice in a bowl in center of ring. (This rice ring goes well with beans, stir-fried vegetables, or any dish that is served over rice.)
Makes 10 servings. 186 calories, 1.2 g fat, 403 mg sodium.

Vegetable Rice 2

• DONNA GREEN GOODMAN

  2 tablespoons olive oil
  ⅓ cup fresh cilantro
  ½ cup cabbage, shredded

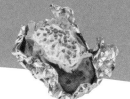

1 large carrot, chopped
½ cup chopped sweet pepper, red and green
½ cup chopped mushrooms
1 small onion, chopped
2 cups instant brown rice
2 cups hot water
1 tablespoon McKay's Chicken Style Seasoning (without MSG)

In large skillet (preferably iron) sauté vegetable and cilantro until crisp tender. Add dry rice and stir-fry for approximately one minute. Add hot water and McKay's Chicken Style Seasoning. Bring to boil. Lower and let steam until rice is done (about 10-15 minutes).
Makes 6 servings. 130 calories, 4 g fat, 8 mg sodium.

Yellow Rice (Africa)
• PAMELA WILLIAMS

4 cups boiling water
2 cups long-grain brown rice
½ teaspoon ground cinnamon
⅛ teaspoon saffron
1 tablespoon butter
½ teaspoon turmeric
4 tablespoons raw sugar
3 tablespoons seedless raisins

Add all the ingredients except raisins to the water and cook over low heat for 40 minutes. Stir in raisins and cook for an additional 10 minutes or until liquid is absorbed. Serve immediately.
Makes 4 servings. 215 calories, 3.5 g fat, 281 mg sodium.

Coconut Ginger Rice
• PAMELA AND ERMA WILLIAMS

Vegetable oil spray
1 large onion, thinly sliced
1 teaspoon fresh ginger
2 cups instant brown rice, uncooked
2¼ cups water

2 teaspoons McKay's Chicken Style Seasoning
⅔ cup grated coconut
2 tablespoons fresh parsley, minced

Spray vegetable oil in a nonstick skillet. Sauté onion until soft. Add ginger, rice, water, and McKay's Chicken Style Seasoning, stirring constantly. Cover pan and let simmer over low heat for 5 minutes. Stir in coconut and continue to cook until rice is tender. Add parsley. Serve at once.
Makes 6 servings. 123 calories, 3 g fat, 623 mg sodium.

Coconut Rice
• PAMELA AND ERMA WILLIAMS

6 scallions, chopped
1 tablespoon pine nuts
⅓ cup unsweetened shredded coconut
1 tablespoon oil
2½ cups water
1 tablespoon coconut milk
1 teaspoon salt
1½ cups brown rice

Sauté scallions, pine nuts, and coconut in oil until nuts are lightly toasted and scallions are lightly limp. Add water, coconut milk, and salt. Bring to a boil, and stir in rice. Cook 40 minutes until rice is tender. Let set 10 minutes and serve.
Makes 6 servings. 86 calories, 5 g fat.

Saffron Rice (India)

• PAT HUMPHREY

- ¾ teaspoon saffron (turmeric)
- 2 cups water, flavored with 1 teaspoon McKay's Chicken Style Seasoning
- 3 tablespoons margarine
- 1 large onion, finely sliced
- 1 cup brown rice
- 1 clove garlic, crushed
- 4 whole cloves
- ¼ teaspoon cardamom
- ¼ cup cashews or slivered almonds, toasted
- ¼ cup golden raisins

Soak saffron in ¼ cup broth made with McKay's Chicken Style Seasoning for 1 hour. Strain and reserve saffron liquid. Heat margarine in heavy 2-quart oven-proof kettle. Add onion and rice and sauté, stirring constantly, until rice becomes straw-colored. Stir in 1 cup of broth. Add dash of salt to taste, garlic, cloves, and cardamom. Cover kettle, transfer to 400° F oven and bake 20 minutes or until rice absorbs all liquid. Stir once with a fork. Heat remaining broth and add to rice. Cover, reduce heat to 200° F and bake 10 to 15 minutes more. Remove cover, add nuts and raisins, and toss with fork. Leave in oven uncovered 4 to 5 minutes.
Makes 8 servings. 208 calories, 8.8 g fat, 20 mg sodium.

Philippine Fried Rice (Oriental)

• PAT HUMPHREY

- 3 cups brown rice, uncooked
- 1 medium green pepper
- 2 medium onions
- 3 tomatoes
- 2 stalks celery
- 3 tablespoons butter
  Dash salt
- 2 teaspoons fried rice seasoning

Cook rice according to package directions. Chop all vegetables finely, and in a wok or skillet, sauté in butter until tender. Add salt and seasoning, then add rice and fry approximately 5 minutes.
Makes 8 servings. 326 calories, 6 g fat, 60 mg sodium.

Risi e Bisi (Rice and Green Peas) (Italy)

• PAT HUMPHREY

- 2 tablespoons chicken-style seasoning
- 2 cups water
- 1 medium yellow onion, chopped fine
- 2 teaspoons light margarine
- ⅔ cup 30-minute brown rice
- ½ cup fresh or frozen green peas

Mix chicken-style seasoning with water to make chicken-style broth, then heat in small saucepan. Sauté onion in skillet with half the margarine for about 5 minutes. Add the rice and peas, and cook 2 minutes longer. Add chicken-style broth, reduce heat, and cook until liquid is absorbed (about 20 minutes).
Makes 4 servings: 174 calories, 3 g fat, 51 mg sodium.

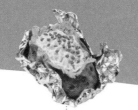

Quick Bread Dressing
• PAMELA AND ERMA WILLIAMS

1	medium onion, chopped
4	tablespoons margarine
1	teaspoon sage
½	teaspoon thyme
1	can cream of mushroom soup
½	can evaporated milk
8 to 10	slices of toasted bread, cubed

Brown chopped onion in margarine. Add sage, thyme, mushroom soup, and milk. Pour over bread cubes. Mix and pour into greased baking dish. Cover and bake at 325° F for one hour.

Makes 8 servings. 182 calories, 7 g fat.

Desserts

For some, the best part of the meal is the dessert—a freshly baked brownie that melts in your mouth or a decadent fruit dessert with raspberry sauce drizzled on top. Here, the finest blend of fruits and other delicious ingredients are combined to help create the best part of the meal. Experience the unique blend of warm berries and dumplings with a scoop of French vanilla ice cream, or enjoy a bite of apple crisp with a steaming cup of hot tea. These recipes provide an array of flavors that will add the perfect final touch to any meal.

Banana Nut Cookies
• PAMELA WILLIAMS

1 cup oats
1 cup wheat flour
⅓ cup oil
1 ripe banana, mashed
½ cup apple juice
¼ cup chopped walnuts
½ cup chopped dates

Mix oats and flour. Stir in oil. Add mashed bananas and apple juice, then nuts and dates. Drop by spoonfuls onto oiled cookie sheet. Bake at 350° F for 30 minutes.
Makes 30 servings. 56 calories, 2 g fat, 0 mg sodium.

Peanut Butter Cookies
• DONNA GREEN GOODMAN

¾ cup honey
2 teaspoons alcohol-free vanilla
¾ teaspoon salt
½ teaspoon alcohol-free lemon extract
1½ cups peanut butter
¼ cup oil
1 cup whole wheat pastry
1 cup oat flour
½ teaspoon baking powder (aluminum/ baking soda free-featherweight)

In bowl mix all ingredients together well. Form into small balls and place on cookie sheet. Flatten with fork. Bake at 350° F for 12 to 15 minutes. Watch carefully.
Makes 15 servings. 146 calories, 8 g fat, 115 mg sodium.
VARIATION: Add carob chips.

Fat content can be lowered by choosing nonfat or low-fat pie crusts, milk, or yogurt, and eliminating the nuts in some of the recipes. In addition, various sweeteners are available which can be used in place of sugar—honey, maple syrup, and juice or juice concentrates.

Desserts

Oatmeal and Raisin Cookies (KIDS)
• PAMELA AND ERMA WILLIAMS

½ cup wheat germ
½ cup soy flour
2½ cups rolled oats
1 tablespoon baking yeast
½ teaspoon salt
¼ teaspoon cinnamon
½ cup raisins
⅔ cup molasses
⅓ cup oil
2 eggs (or egg substitute equivalent)
½ cup apple juice
1 teaspoon vanilla
Nonstick cooking spray

Combine dry ingredients and raisins. Beat together molasses, oil, eggs, apple juice, and vanilla. Add to dry ingredients and mix thoroughly. Spray cookie sheet with nonstick cooking spray and drop mixture by spoonfuls onto cookie sheet. Bake at 375° F for 12 to 15 minutes.
Makes 20 cookies. 89 calories, 1 g fat.

Carob Crispy Cookies
• PAMELA AND ERMA WILLIAMS

2 egg whites, (see substitute p. 19) unbeaten
¾ cups maple syrup
1½ tablespoons carob powder
4 cups puffed rice cereal
1 teaspoon almond extract
½ teaspoon vanilla extract
4 tablespoons crushed walnuts

Preheat oven to 300° F. In a bowl, beat egg whites until soft peaks form. Slowly add maple syrup and beat until egg whites are stiff. Gently stir in carob powder, cereal, nuts, almond extract, and vanilla extract. Spray cookie sheet with non-stick spray. Drop batter by tablespoon onto cookie sheet. Bake for 30 minutes or until cookies are light brown. Cool on wire rack. Serve.
Makes 40 cookies. 35 calories, 0 g fat.

Almond Cookies
• PAMELA AND ERMA WILLIAMS

1½ cups almonds
½ cup honey
3 ripe bananas, peeled and mashed
1 cup whole wheat pastry flour
1½ cups unbleached white flour
1 teaspoon almond extract

Preheat oven to 350° F. In a food processor grind 1 cup of almonds into a meal. In a separate, large bowl cream the honey and mashed bananas. Add almond meal and flours. Mix well. Divide and roll dough into 20 balls. Press 1 whole almond onto each cookie. Bake in vegetable-oil-sprayed pan at 350° F for 12 minutes. Remove from oven and cool.
Makes 20 cookies. 137 calories, 2.4 g fat.

Walnut Brownies
• PAMELA WILLIAMS

½ cup honey
¼ cup oil
1 2½-ounce jar prune baby food puree
¼ cup soy milk
1 ¼ teaspoons vanilla
1 cup whole wheat pastry flour
⅓ cup unsweetened carob powder
2 teaspoons soy flour
½ teaspoon cinnamon
¼ teaspoon salt
½ cup chopped walnuts

Preheat oven to 325° F. Combine honey, oil, prune puree, soy milk, and vanilla in food processor and blend well. In a separate bowl combine whole wheat flour, carob powder, soy flour, cinnamon, and salt. Add to oil mixture and gently stir until ingredients are evenly moistened. Stir in nuts. Spread mixture in an 8-inch-square nonstick pan. Bake until firm, about 25 minutes. Cool and cut into squares.
Makes 16 two-inch squares. 110 calories, 5.5 g fat, 38 mg sodium.

Caro-Brownies
• PAMELA AND ERMA WILLIAMS

  1½ cups rice flour
   1 cup carob powder
  ¼ teaspoon salt
  ½ cup chopped walnuts
   1 10-ounce package soft silken tofu
   1 teaspoon vanilla extract
  ½ cup barley malt
  ⅓ cup maple syrup
   1 cup low-fat milk
  ⅓ cup prunes, pitted, cooked until soft and drained, or prune baby food puree

Preheat oven to 350° F. In a bowl combine first three ingredients. In a blender puree the rest of the ingredients, except walnuts, until smooth. Slowly add ingredients in bowl with the first three ingredients, whisking together until thoroughly mixed. Mix in walnuts. Pour into a lightly oiled 8" x 8" baking pan and bake 30 minutes. Cool. Top with fruit spread or frosting (optional). Cut into squares and serve.
Makes 12 servings. 295 calories, 3.3 g fat.

Chillin Chunkies
• BARBARA FRAZIER

  ¾ cup carob powder
  ½ cup low-fat chunky peanut butter, with no added salt
  ¼ cup honey
  ½ cup dates, chopped
  ¾ cup walnuts
  ⅓ cup sunflower seeds
     Vegetable oil cooking spray

Mix carob powder and peanut butter in two quart saucepan over low heat, until well blended. Add dates, nuts, and seeds. Combine thoroughly. Spoon mixture into 8-inch square dish, lightly sprayed with cooking spray. Chill outdoors in a protected area. Cut into squares and serve, or wrap individual servings in plastic wrap for later use.
Makes 20 servings. 121 calories, 11 g fat, 4 g protein, 1.3 mg sodium.

Oatmeal Squares
• PAT HUMPHREY

   4 cups of oats
   1 cup coconut
  1½ cups whole wheat flour
   1 cup brown sugar
   1 teaspoon salt
   1 cup raisins or dates
   1 cup nuts chopped
   1 cup nut butter
   1 cup carob chips

Mix all ingredients, adding a little water for consistency. Press into oiled pan to one-half inch thickness. Bake at 350° F for 35 minutes.
Makes 16 servings. 411 calories, 17 g fat, 189 mg sodium.

Oatmeal Date Bars
• PAT HUMPHREY

- 1 cup walnuts
- ½ cup orange juice
- ½ cup flaked coconut
- 2 tablespoons honey
- ½ cup whole wheat flour
- ½ cup white flour
- 1 teaspoon orange rind
- 2 cups quick oats
- ½ teaspoon salt
- 2 cups dates
- 2 cups crushed pineapple
- 2 cups pineapple juice
- ½ teaspoon lemon extract

Topping: Blend walnuts, orange juice, coconut, and honey in blender until fine. Add flour, orange rind, oats, and salt. Mix gently with fork until crumbly. Set aside. *Filling:* Simmer dates and pineapple with pineapple juice until dates are tender. Place half of topping into 8-inch-square baking dish. Layer filling on top and then cover with remaining topping. Bake at 350° F for 30 minutes. Then uncover and bake for an additional 15 minutes. Cool and slice into bars.
Makes 9 servings. 392 calories, 10.9 g fat, 131 mg sodium.

Peanut Candy
• PAMELA WILLIAMS

- 3 tablespoons molasses
- 1 tablespoon honey
- ⅓ cup peanut butter
- 2 tablespoons peanuts, chopped
- ½ cup tofu milk powder

Thoroughly mix molasses, honey, peanut butter, and peanuts. Gradually stir the tofu milk powder and blend together. Dust board with dry milk powder. Roll mixture into a long rope, about 1 inch in diameter. Cut into 1-inch pieces.
Makes 15 servings: 81 calories, 4 g fat, 69 mg sodium.

Crunchy Banana Lollipops (KIDS)
• PAMELA AND ERMA WILLIAMS

- 3 firm ripe bananas
- 6 popsicle sticks
- 1 cup presweetened, low-fat strawberry yogurt
- 1 cup chopped nuts

Cover a cookie sheet with wax paper. Peel bananas and cut across the middle in two halves. Put popsicle sticks in the center of each halved banana. Brush bananas with presweetened yogurt. Roll in chopped nuts. Place on cookie sheet. Place in freezer for 30 minutes until firm. (Carob syrup can be used in place of yogurt.)
Makes 6 servings. 203 calories, 11 g fat.

Carob Halva (Near East)
• PAT HUMPHREY

- ½ cup tahini (sesame seed butter)
- 1-2 tablespoons carob powder
- ¼ cup honey
- ⅓ cup sunflower or sesame seed meal (grind in dry blender)

Mix ingredients well and roll into small balls about an inch in diameter. Or shape into a large mound for slicing. Refrigerate (can also be frozen). Variation: Add carob powder last, mixing in lightly for a marble-like effect.
Makes 12 servings. 90 calories, 6 g fat, 2 mg sodium.

Popcorn Balls
• PAMELA WILLIAMS

- 1 cup honey
- 3 cups popcorn, popped but unbuttered
- ⅓ cup walnuts or pecans, chopped

In a skillet, bring honey to a slow boil for two minutes. Stir in popcorn and nuts. When cool, form into small balls. Place on wax paper until ready to eat.
Makes 8 servings. 184 calories, 4 g fat, 2 mg sodium.

Coconut Bonbons
• PAMELA WILLIAMS

- ¾ cup tofu milk powder
- ½ cup shredded coconut
- 1 slice dried pineapple, finely chopped
- 3 tablespoons molasses
- 1 tablespoon honey
- ¾ cup crushed crispy rice cereal
- 2 tablespoons shredded coconut

Mix tofu milk powder, coconut, and pineapple in a bowl. Add molasses and honey and mix well. Shape into 1-inch balls. Mix crushed rice cereal and shredded coconut. Roll balls in cereal coconut mixture.
Makes 15 servings. 71 calories, 1 g fat, 79 mg sodium.

Carob Delights
• PAT HUMPHREY

- 1 cup unsweetened coconut
- ½ cup carob powder
- 1 cup Better Than Milk powder
- ½ cup honey
- 2 teaspoons vanilla
  Dash of salt
- 1 tablespoon water

Mix all ingredients well (mixture will be thick). Shape into 1-inch balls and refrigerate. If desired, you can roll balls in coconut before refrigerating.
Makes 24 servings. 58 calories, 2.3 g fat, 59 mg sodium.

Kiwi-Berry Bisque
• DONNA A. SMITH

- 1 cup rice milk or soy milk
- 6 kiwi, peeled
- 1 16-ounce bag frozen strawberries
- 4 bananas
- 2 15-ounce cans sliced peaches in juice (do not drain)

- ⅓ cup fructose
- 1 teaspoon cardamom
  Slivered almonds
  Shredded coconut

Puree milk, kiwi, strawberries, and two bananas. Pour pureed mixture over sliced bananas, peaches, and remaining strawberries. Add fructose and cardamom seasoning. Garnish with slivered almonds and coconut shreds.
Makes 6 servings. 226 calories, 0 g fat, 0 mg sodium.

Tofu Ice Cream

- 1 10-ounce package soft silken tofu
- ½ cup maple syrup
- 2 tablespoons arrowroot powder
- 4-6 teaspoons vanilla
- 1 teaspoon guar gum
  dash of salt

Combine all the ingredients in a food processor and blend until smooth. Freeze solid. Defrost for 10 minutes and place in food processor. Mix again until smooth and freeze a second time. Remove from the freezer and serve. Top with bananas and strawberries, granola, or nuts.
Makes 4 servings. 161 calories, 4.4g fat.

Banana Ice
• PAMELA AND ERMA WILLIAMS

  1 large ripe banana
     Shredded coconut

Peel the banana and slice into one-inch thick pieces. Place in large plastic covered container and freeze. Puree in a blender or food processor. As the banana thaws, the texture will become smooth. Place in a serving dish and top with shredded coconut. Serve.
Makes 2 servings. 100 calories, 1 g fat.

Carob Almond Pudding

  1 10-ounce package silken soft tofu
  ⅓ cup carob powder
  ¼ cup maple syrup
  2 tablespoons smooth almond butter
  1 teaspoon almond extract

Place all ingredients in a blender or food processor. Puree until smooth. Chill in individual custard cups and garnish with a sprig of fresh mint or slivered almonds.
Makes 6 servings. 204 calories, 4.3 fat.

Banana Pudding
• PAMELA AND ERMA WILLIAMS

  1 10-ounce package soft silken tofu
  2 very ripe bananas
  1 teaspoon vanilla extract
  ¼ cup maple syrup
  4-5 drops fresh lemon juice

Blend ingredients in a blender until smooth. Serve immediately.
Makes 4 servings. 160 calories, 0 g fat.

Peach Crunch
• PAMELA AND IRMA WILLIAMS

  3 cups sliced unsweetened peaches (fresh, frozen, or canned)
  1 cup raisins
  2 tablespoons shredded coconut
  ¼ teaspoon nutmeg
  ⅓ cup prepared granola
  ⅓ cup oats
  2 tablespoons oil
  3 tablespoons water

Preheat oven to 375° F. Arrange peach slices in an 8" x 8" baking dish. Sprinkle with raisins, cinnamon, and nutmeg. In a bowl combine remaining ingredients. Mixture should be crumbly. Sprinkle granola mixture over peaches and raisins evenly. Bake for 30 minutes until peaches are tender. Serve warm or cold, or with tofu ice cream.
Makes 8 servings. 124 calories, 3.2 g fat.

Baked Cinnamon Apples
• PAMELA AND ERMA WILLIAMS

  4 medium to large McIntosh or Rome apples
  ¾ cup golden raisins
  ¼ cup chopped pecans
  2 tablespoons peanut butter
  1 tablespoon brown sugar
  ½ teaspoon cinnamon
  ½ teaspoon vanilla extract
  ½ cup apple juice
  4 tablespoons apple butter

Preheat oven to 375° F. Core apples and pierce with fork around the center. Mix raisins, nuts, peanut butter, cinnamon, brown sugar, apple butter, cinnamon, brown sugar, apple butter, and vanilla in a mixing bowl. Place mixture in the center of each apple. Place apples in a glass baking dish and pour apple juice into pan. Cover with foil and bake 30 minutes until tender.
Makes 4 servings. 198 calories, 15.8 g fat.

Easy Apple Crisp

    4 apples, peeled and cut in wedges
    1 can crushed pineapple
    1½ cups low-fat granola

Place apples in baking dish. Cover with crushed pineapple and top with granola. Bake at 350° F for about 20 minutes or until thoroughly heated.
Makes 4 servings. 305 calories, 6 g fat, 130 mg sodium.

Tropical Pears

• PAMELA AND ERMA WILLIAMS
    ¾ cup pineapple juice
    ¾ cup orange juice
    2 tablespoons coconut milk
    3 tablespoons honey
    1 tablespoon lemon juice
    3-4 lemon slices
    ¼ teaspoon grated orange rind
    2 large fresh pears, peeled, halved, and core removed
       Shredded coconut

Put pineapple juice, orange juice, coconut milk, honey, lemon slices, and orange rind into a skillet. Place pear halves in juice. Cover and simmer until pears are just tender. Sprinkle with coconut and add a peppermint leaf for garnish.
Makes 6 servings. 115 calories, 1 g fat.

Tropical Banana Split

• PAMELA AND ERMA WILLIAMS
    ½ cup ricotta cheese, cottage cheese, or nonfat yogurt
    2 teaspoons bran
    1 teaspoon honey
    2 tablespoons chopped pineapple
    1 tablespoon coconut
    1 jar strawberry topping
    1 tablespoon granola
    1 firm ripe banana

Cut banana in half lengthwise and place in a bowl as with a banana split. Combine the ricotta cheese (or cottage cheese or yogurt) with the bran and next three ingredients and place a scoop in the middle of the banana halves. Spoon strawberry topping over the cheese and sprinkle with granola.
Makes 1 serving. 365 calories, (lower with nonfat yogurt), 12 g fat.
VARIATION: Top with ripe mango or papaya.)

Pears and Raspberries

• PAMELA WILLIAMS
    4 large fresh pears
    3 cups water
    1 cinnamon stick
    3 whole cloves
    4 tablespoons honey
    6 tablespoons plain nonfat yogurt
    1 tablespoon lemon juice
    1 cup fresh or frozen raspberries

Peel pears. Cut in half and remove core. In a saucepan combine water, cinnamon, cloves, and 2 tablespoons honey and bring to boil. Add pears and simmer for 10 minutes. Remove pears. Mix yogurt, lemon juice, and 1 tablespoon honey. Fill pear halves with yogurt mixture. Place two pear halves together to make a whole pear and stand upright in a serving dish. If necessary, cut a small slice from the bottom of the pear to make it stand. Puree ½ cup of raspberries with 1 tablespoon honey. Pour puree over pears and garnish with the other ½ cup of raspberries. Sprinkle with ground cinnamon.
Makes 4 servings. 204 calories, 1 g fat, 16 mg sodium.

Desserts

Holiday Fruit Cake

   1 pound whole pitted dates, chopped
   1 pound shelled walnuts, chopped
   1 cup whole wheat flour, sifted
   ½ teaspoon salt
   ¼ cup raisins
   1 cup honey
   4 eggs, yolks separated from whites
   1 teaspoon vanilla

Combine dates, walnuts, flour, and salt in a mixing bowl. Add raisins, honey, well-beaten egg yolks, and vanilla. Then carefully fold in egg whites that have been beaten dry. Turn into two small bread pans lined with oiled paper. Bake for one hour at 350° F. Makes 20 servings. 160 calories, 4.6 g fat.

Pumpkin Coconut Cream Pie

• PAMELA AND ERMA WILLIAMS.

   1½ cups cooked mashed pumpkin
   3 eggs (or egg substitute equivalent), beaten
   ¼ cup honey
   ½ teaspoon salt
   ¾ cup toasted coconut
   ½ cup chopped pecans
   2 cups milk

Combine pumpkin and eggs and beat well. Add honey, salt, coconut, and nuts. Mix well. Add milk and mix. Turn into unbaked 9-inch shell. Bake at 400° F for one hour. Chill and serve.
Makes 8 servings. 138 calories, 6 g fat.

INDEX TO INTERNATIONAL RECIPES

Have you ever wanted to take a trip around the world? Well, now you can—from the comfort of your kitchen. From Africa, to the Caribbean, to Mexico, to Asia, these ethnic vegetarian culinary delights are sure to please even the most particular palates. Bon voyage!

Africa

Each African country has its own unique blend of spices, fruits, vegetables, nuts, legumes, grains, and protein sources. Some of the staples of African cuisine include groundnuts or peanuts, yams, corn, coconut, spicy sauces, and stews. For a splendid taste of Africa, try a few of these recipes at your next festive dinner.

Australia

Caribbean

These exotic dishes serve up a special blend of fruit, peas, nuts , and spices for a memorable culinary experience. Although most Caribbean cuisine finds its roots in Africa, India, Europe, and South America, it offers a unique and exciting flavor. So come and indulge in a taste of the tropical islands.

Europe

Oriental

Italy

If you enjoy the distinctive flavor of Italian food, you'll like this collection of recipes—from sauces to main dishes to salads. Our heart-healthy recipes are packed with nutrition, yet low in fat, cholesterol, and calories. So go ahead—eat to your heart's content!

Mexico

Near East

South America

From the Andes Mountains to the coastal towns, South America offers a diverse and delectable cuisine. The varied climates allow for the growth of a wide variety of fruits, vegetables, grains, and a host of meats and seafood. These recipes offer a taste of this rich cuisine—vegetarian style.

INDEX TO SPECIAL OCCASION RECIPES

Christmas Dinner

Indulging in culinary festivities with family and friends is usually the highlight of the holiday season. Herbs and spices enhance the flavor of food without destroying nutritive value or adding unnecessary calories. So entertain this holiday season with herbs and spices that make your holiday meal healthy and tasty! Here's a selection of special recipes to use in planning your holiday menus.

Easter Brunch

A brunch is always a great idea for fun, fellowship, and delicious food. Imagine a bright spring morning with some of our tasty selections spread out before the guests. Be sure to include cheery seasonal flowers on your table settings. These menus are perfect for a Mother's Day brunch too.

Elegant Dinner

Your finest dinnerware, a floral arrangement, candles, and your best silverware all combine to create an elegant ambience. Plan your menu from these delicious recipes, and you'll have created a memorable dinner.

Broccoli Salad, p. 64
Carob Almond Pudding, p. 130
Eggplant Caviar, p. 67
Greek Spinach Salad, p. 60
Herbal Lemon Dressing, p. 69
Miso Soup, p. 32
Orange Acorn Squash, p. 108
Pears and Raspberries, p. 131
Quick Skillet Steak, p. 94
Sesame Green Beans, p. 116
Spanish Rice, p. 103
Tropical Mint-aide, p. 57
Zucchini Quiche, p. 79

Festive Party

Whether it's a lively Saturday night gathering or a formal dinner for two, be sure to include a selection from our enticing finger foods.

Banana Nut Cookies, p. 125
Black Bean Dip, p. 41
Eggplant Pizza, p. 43
Greek Spinach Turnovers, p. 44
Petite Meatless Corned Beef Puffs, p. 44
Spinach Paté, p. 42
Stuffed Cherry Tomatoes, p. 41
Stuffed Grape Leaves, p. 42
Stuffed Zucchini, p. 43
Tofu Kabobs, p. 42
Tofu Spread, p. 44
Vegetable Fondue, p. 43

Thanksgiving Dinner

Holiday time creates memories full of love, laughter,
and good food. Family gathered around the table, heads bowed, giving thanks for the blessings of the year and the good food before them. Vegetarian roast turkey. Pumpkin coconut cream pie. These and other recipes will provide delicious memories!

Coconut Rice, p. 121
Cranberry Orange Relish, p. 75
Greek Spinach Salad, p. 60
Italian Zucchini, p. 116
Mixed Greens and Watercress Salad, p. 60
Mock Turkey Loaf, p. 83
Mushroom and Vegetable Casserole, p. 111
Orange Acorn Squash, p. 108
Pumpkin Coconut Cream Pie, p. 132
Quick Break Dressing, p. 123
Sweet Potato Balls, p. 119
Vegetarian Roast, p. 92
Vegetarian Roast Turkey, p. 94
Waldorf Salad, p. 70

Kids' Party

Satisfy the munchies of any group of hungry kids on a game night, birthday party, sleepover or any other celebration they dream up. Pick from our easy, healthy, kid-tested choices and they'll pick you as MVP (Most Valuable Parent)!

Chik Nuggets, p. 41
Crunchy Banana Lollipops, p. 128
Egg Salad Sandwich Filling, p. 45
Fast 'n' Easy Bean Soup, p. 29
Gingerbread, p. 20
Oatmeal and Raisin Cookies, p. 126
Oven Baked Fries, p. 48
Peanut Candy, p. 128
Pineapple Breakfast Cookies, p. 12
Tofu Burgers With Cheese, p. 47
Tofu Ice Cream, p. 129
Veggie Big Boy, p. 46
Watermelon Slush, p. 56

GENERAL INDEX

Index

We'd like to bring some important issues to your attention.

VIOLENCE. RACISM. EDUCATION. MONEY. MARRIAGE.

These are the hot issues in your community and the issues we grapple with in MESSAGE magazine. The advantage of MESSAGE is that it brings the Bible into the discussion. You get a sense of hope and a depth of understanding you won't find anywhere else. Subscribe to MESSAGE. You'll find that every issue of MESSAGE connects with an important issue in your life.

MESSAGE

Call 1-800-765-6955 to order
www.messagemagazine.org

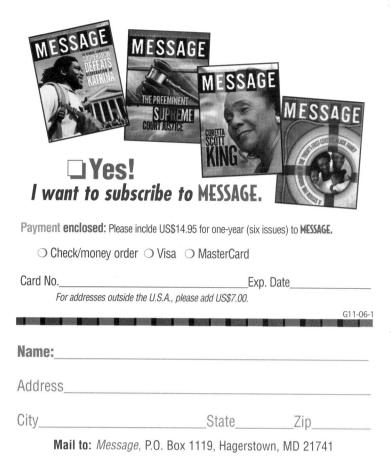

☐ Yes!
I want to subscribe to MESSAGE.

Payment enclosed: Please inclde US$14.95 for one-year (six issues) to **MESSAGE**.

○ Check/money order   ○ Visa   ○ MasterCard

Card No._____ Exp. Date_____
For addresses outside the U.S.A., please add US$7.00.

G11-06-1

Name:_____

Address_____

City_____ **State**_____ **Zip**_____

Mail to: *Message*, P.O. Box 1119, Hagerstown, MD 21741

Share **Good Health**

Mail to:

Subscriber Services
P.O. Box 1119
Hagerstown, MD 21741
Call 1-800-765-6955
or visit www.vibrantlife.com

"Buy One, Share One Free"

Tell your friends, coworkers, family members, or neighbors that you've found valuable secrets for:

✔ **Losing** weight
✔ **Eating** smarter
✔ **Exercising** effectively
✔ **Finding** peace of mind
✔ **Knowing** God better

Vibrant Life
M A G A Z I N E

Surprise them with a gift subscription to *Vibrant Life*. They'll recognize right away that you care about their health and happiness. ● Order one subscription to *Vibrant Life* for US$20.00 (one year, six issues), then send a second subscription anywhere in the U.S.A. for **FREE**!

Please add US$7.00 for each address outside the U.S.A. Offer subject to change.

Don't wait. Order a gift subscription today!

Send subscriptions to:

Your name_____

Address_____

City_____ State_____ Zip_____

Phone_____

Gift name_____

Address_____

City_____ State_____ Zip_____

Phone_____

F05-02-0

Celebrate
Good Health!

Give yourself a gift that will keep on giving—a happy, healthy lifestyle.

THE OPTIMAL DIET: *THE OFFICIAL CHIP COOKBOOK RECIPES TO REVERSE AND PREVENT DISEASE*

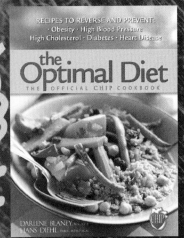

Darlene P. Blaney and Hans A. Diehl The successful lifestyle-improvement program CHIP, the Coronary Health Improvement Project, has now released a collection of their best recipes. Built on the goodness of natural foods, these delicious recipes will reverse and prevent obesity and disease. 978-0-8127-0437-2. Wire-O, 166 pages. **US$14.99**

SEVEN SECRETS COOKBOOK
HEALTHY CUISINE YOUR FAMILY WILL LOVE

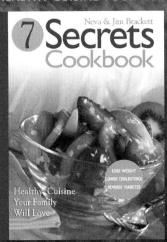

Neva and Jim Brackett For 10 years the authors owned and operated restaurants at which they served delicious, healthful food. In this cookbook they share nearly 200 recipes and the seven secrets that make healthy food taste fabulous. 0-8280-1995-9. Wire-O, 124 pages. **US$14.99**

CREATION HEALTH BREAKTHROUGH

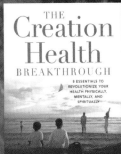

Monica Reed, MD, with Donna K. Wallace. Dr. Monica Reed prescribes eight powerful and scientifically proven essentials to reverse the negative effects of lifestyle, prevent disease, and ultimately achieve total health and wellness. Hardcover, 271 pages. 978-0-446-57762-5. **US$22.99**

HIGH PERFORMANCE HEALTH

James M. Rippe, M.D. World-renowned cardiologist Dr. James Rippe lays out an easy-to-understand blueprint for wellness that includes such principles as eating to fuel performance, establishing a time for solitude, and embracing active rest principles. 978-0-8499-0182-9. Hardcover, 229 pages. **US$24.99**

PAIN FREE FOR LIFE

Scott C. Brady, MD, with William Proctor The founder of Florida Hospital's Brady Institute for Health shares for the first time with the general public his six-week cure for chronic pain. He addresses "impossible to cure" pains and offers dramatic solutions that do not require surgery or drugs. 978-0-446-57761-8. Hardcover, 288 pages. **US$23.99**